Copyright Basic Living LLC All Rights

No part of this publication may be reproduced, distributed in any form or by any means, electronic or mechanical, or stored in a database or retrieval system, without prior written permission from the author.

The information included in this eBook is for entertainment purposes only. The publisher, author, and contributors of this eBook are not responsible in any manner whatsoever for any adverse effects arising directly or indirectly as a result of the information provided in this book.

Book design and layout by Basic Living LLC.

For more recipe inspiration, visit
www.basiclivingbr.com

BASIC NUTRITION
A NOTE FROM

Eating healthy is important each day – even on days when lunch is in a box! Packing a healthy lunch box for children can be easy if you plan. Here are some guidelines, safety tips, and nutritious ideas.

Eat at least:
1. One serving of vegetables or salad AND one serving of fruit
2. One serving of protein such as chicken, fish OR meat alternative such as eggs, beans, hummus, cheese, yogurt, peanut butter or cottage cheese
3. One serving of 1% or fat-free milk AND water
4. A grain product such as bread, bagel, muffin, roll, crackers, or tortilla

By including each of these in your child's lunch, you will not only make sure that they have a nutritious lunch but that they don't end up hungry after they get back to class.

1. Chill food thoroughly before packing.
2. Pack meals in an insulated bag.
3. Pack foods with the items used first in the bag last.
4. Keep food safety supplies such as hand sanitizer and disinfectant wipes, or paper towels and spray cleanser.

HOW TO PACK A HEALTHY LUNCH

It's so easy to get in a rut of making the same thing day after day, week after week and your brain just can't think past the usual peanut butter and jelly sandwich, chips, and a juice box. But packing the same old food into that lunch box every day can get boring!

We've put together more than 100 healthy lunch box ideas so you never have to think too hard about what to pack.

Kids are much more likely to eat healthy foods when they are away from home if they are used to eating healthy foods at home on a regular basis, it becomes part of their routine. If your child is a picky eater, try adding new healthy foods into the family diet on a regular basis and make it fun.

If you aren't sure what your children like to eat for lunch, open their lunch boxes when they get home from school. The food that doesn't get eaten will likely give you some insight into what your kids will and won't eat.

7 TIPS

1. **Plan for lunches.** When cooking dinner, you can make extra and separate them into lunch-size portions for the freezer. This will save you hassle on days you are running late. This is also a great way to save money as well. Write down and schedule all of your lunch boxes ahead of time so you don't have to think about it at the last minute!

2. **Buy reusable containers.** (Bento Box) Separated containers are a great option but you can also use silicone cupcake molds in various sizes to make your own compartments for lunches. Reusable containers are great for keeping lunches fresh and preventing messy spills. Our favorite style boxes are Bento Boxes.

3. **Save condiment packets** when your family eats out to place in lunch boxes for easy lunch packing. If you don't collect packages while out you can fill small containers with condiments of school lunches. Or you can easily purchase condiment packets online. For sandwiches, you can put mustard between slices of deli meat and cheese to keep the bread from getting soggy.

4. **Use cookie cutters** to give foods fun shapes without a lot of extra work. You can find bulk packs of cookie cutters for cheap and plenty of variety. Amazon has a large selection to choose from. You can make it fun with new themes each day. Sandwiches, tortillas, baked goods, and fruits can all be shaped for a fun lunch in no time.

5. **Create a basket filled with pre-packed snacks** and sides for lunches. These could be zip lock bags that you pre-fill with bulk purchases of chips or crackers. Or, you can save yourself time and buy an assortment of snacks ready to toss in the lunch box. Then you can just toss them into the lunch box and be done. You can pre-make the refrigerated parts of lunches on Sunday afternoon, as well, so they are ready to go.

6. **Freeze foods** that freeze and thaw well so your child's lunch can act as its own ice pack. Sandwiches, yogurts, and most main dishes can be frozen fully cooked, and ready to go for school lunches. Freezing drinks is another easy idea to keep lunches cold. Or use cold packs to keep food cool during the school day; they work really well.

7. **Plan balanced meals** by ensuring your lunches each has protein, grain, fruit or veggie, and dairy.

LUNCHBOX HACKS
EVERY PARENT NEEDS

1. Freeze peanut butter sandwiches and let them thaw in the lunch box. You can make your own version of Uncrustables.

2. Freeze a wet sponge inside a zip-top baggie to make your own ice pack that you can reuse.

3. Use drinks as ice packs. Fill a water bottle 1/3 full and freeze, remove from freezer and fill with water to top, and pack ice cold water in the lunch box.

4. Use an apple slicer to pre-cut apples and wrap the apple in plastic wrap to keep the cut apple intact to prevent browning.

5. Make your own single serving packs to save money. Buy a large back of pretzels, or other snacks and divide the contents up into individual baggies.

6. Make your own fruit cups with a plastic container and canned fruit.

7. Wrap sandwiches in wax paper or freezer paper to make a placemat when the paper is opened.

8. Preheat your Thermos to keep hot foods warm longer. All you need to do is pour boiling water into the Thermos and let it sit for a few minutes. Pour out the water and add your hot food.

9. Slice a kiwi in half, wrap in plastic wrap, and pack it in the lunch box with a spoon.

10. Send tomato slices for sandwiches in a plastic baggie to be added to the sandwich at lunchtime.

11. Save plastic take-out containers for disposable lunch boxes when your child needs to take a lunch on a field trip.

12. Make your own Go-Gurts by filling reusable pouches with yogurt. You could also fill them with applesauce.

13. When making sandwiches, place tomato, onions, and lettuce in a separate baggie to prevent the bread from becoming soggy.

TABLE OF CONTENTS

1 BENTO BOX LUNCHES

16 COLD LUNCHES

29 HOT LUNCHES

38 BOWLS

46 SALADS

60 SANDWICHES, WRAPS, & MORE

93 BITE SIZED LUNCHES

As you browse through this book you will notice the recipes are divided into 7 categories. This is to help you select recipes based off personal/child's preference, craving, and occasions when you won't have access to a microwave or heat source. Below is a short summary of each category and the kind of recipes you can expect to find.

BENTO BOXES
Bento boxes are the epitome of a simple lunch that kids will love. The compartmentalized containers allow you to pack a variety of favorite foods, usually 1-2 from every food group.

COLD LUNCHES
Along with bento lunches, options such as quesadillas, deli roll-ups, and parfaits are perfect for days when you know you won't have access to a microwave. Add an ice pack to the lunch bag and you're all set.

HOT LUNCHES
There's nothing like a home-cooked hot lunch to switch up things and this section includes soups, pasta, and loaded potato recipes all of which can be entirely prepped ahead and stored for lunches throughout the week.

BOWLS
Bowls make a balanced and satiating meal with grain for the base and various toppings such as veggies, lean cooked protein, and sauces. It's a no-brainer way to prepare a balanced and nourishing meal that can be enjoyed at room temperature or reheated.

SALADS
These salad recipes prove that there are numerous ways to turn boring, ordinary salads into a full course meal that even the kids will want in on. They are similar to bowls, the only difference is the lettuce or leafy green base instead of a grain. Other than that, pile your base high with lean protein, veggies, and anything else you'd want to be drizzled by your favorite dressing. It's a delicious and relatively low-carb way to fuel up at midday.

SANDWICHES, WRAPS & MORE
A lunch recipe book wouldn't be complete without wraps and sandwiches. This section is by far the densest, packed with all things like grilled cheese, sliders, pitas, and even a few lettuce wraps for all my low-carb lovers.

BITE-SIZED LUNCHES
This section is full of options such as deviled eggs, pinwheels, and mini quiches which are great for prepping ahead and packing into lunch boxes.

WHAT YOU'LL FIND INSIDE

BENTO BOX LUNCHES

1

BASIC NUTRITION
estd. 2020
EAT REAL FOOD

SALMON SALAD

2 servings

INGREDIENTS:
- 2 5-ounce cans of salmon, drained
- 2 tablespoons mayonnaise
- 1/2 cup diced celery
- 1 teaspoon lemon juice
- 1/2 teaspoon cumin
- 1/2 teaspoon salt
- 1/2 teaspoon black pepper
- Whole grain crackers
- 2 apples, sliced

INSTRUCTIONS:
1. In a large bowl, add the salmon meat and use a fork to break up larger pieces into smaller flake-like pieces. Add the mayonnaise, diced celery, lemon juice, cumin, salt, and pepper to the bowl and stir to combine.
2. Divide the salmon salad into 4 lunch containers along with the veggies. Pack the crackers into separate containers to prevent them from getting soggy.

CHICKEN & HUMMUS

2 servings

INGREDIENTS:
- 8 oz grilled chicken breast fillet, sliced 1/2 cup hummus
- 1/2 cup grape tomatoes
- 1/2 medium cucumbers, sliced
- 10-12 black olives
- 2 whole wheat pitas, sliced 1/4 cup feta cheese

INSTRUCTIONS:
1. Evenly divide the sliced chicken, hummus, tomatoes, cucumber, olives, and pita wedges between 2 lunch containers with compartments.
2. Divide the feta cheese between 2 lidded containers and pack with the bistro boxes.

CHICKEN SALAD

2 servings

INGREDIENTS:

Chicken Salad:
- 2 tablespoons lemon juice
- 1/2 cup mayonnaise
- 1/2 teaspoon salt
- 1/4 teaspoon black pepper
- 1 teaspoon cumin
- 3-4 cups shredded rotisserie chicken
- 1/2 cup chopped celery

Bento Boxes:
- 1 1/2 cups Chicken Salad
- 2 apples, sliced Whole grain crackers

INSTRUCTIONS:

1. In a large bowl, combine the lemon juice, mayonnaise, salt, pepper, and cumin, and whisk until thoroughly combined. Add the chicken and fold with a spatula, add the celery and fold again until all the ingredients are fully combined.
2. Evenly divide the chicken salad, sliced apple, and crackers into 2 lunch containers with compartments.

KITCHEN NOTE:
1. *Reserve the remaining chicken salad in an airtight container for up to 3 days.*

BBQ MEATBALLS

1 serving

INGREDIENTS:

- 1 serving meatballs
- bbq dipping sauce for meatballs
- carrot and celery sticks
- apple
- trail mix with chocolate

INSTRUCTIONS:

1. Heat meatballs according to package instructions. Store in a thermos to keep warm or refrigerate until it's time to eat.
2. Pack remaining meal components in your bento box.

KITCHEN NOTE:

1. *Other sauce ideas: bbq sauce, ketchup, peanut sauce, guacamole, ranch dressing, curry sauce*

RAINBOW BOX

2 servings

INGREDIENTS:

- 2 red mini sweet peppers sliced
- 1 Orange
- 1 kiwi sliced
- 1/2 cup sugar snap peas
- 1/4 cup blueberries
- 1/2 cup red seedless grapes
- 1 large spinach wrap
- 2 ounces low-sodium deli-sliced turkey
- 1/2 cup baby spinach chopped
- 1 tablespoon hummus
- 1 slice provolone cheese

INSTRUCTIONS:

1. Assemble lunchboxes with peppers, mandarin, SunGold kiwi, snap peas, blueberries and grapes.
2. Lay wrap on flat surface. Spread with hummus and top with cheese, turkey and spinach. Roll up tightly and slice into 1-inch thick rounds. Add half to each lunchbox.

TUNA SALAD SNACK PACK

2 servings

INGREDIENTS:

- 5 oz. can or pouch of tuna, drained if necessary
- 1 stalk minced celery
- 1 green onion
- 1 Tbsp. mayonnaise
- salt and pepper to taste
- 1 cup Belgian endive leaves
- 1 oz. almonds
- 1 oz. crackers
- 1 cup strawberries

INSTRUCTIONS:

1. Mix together first four ingredients and season with salt and pepper to taste.
2. Wash endive and trim bottom (root section) end so that the leaves split apart.
3. Serve tuna and endive with remaining ingredients on the side. Pack into a bento box.

MANDARIN PASTA SALAD BOX

6 servings

INGREDIENTS:

- 16 ounces rotini pasta
- 6 mini sweet peppers sliced
- 3 Bee Sweet Citrus mandarins peeled, segmented
- 3 green onions sliced
- 2 cups baby spinach chopped
- 1/2 cup matchstick carrots
- 1/2 cup sesame ginger dressing
- 1/4 cup Chow Mein noodles

SIDES PER LUNCHBOX:
- 1 kiwi peeled, sliced
- 1/2 cup steamed edamame pods

INSTRUCTIONS:

1. Cook pasta according to package directions. Drain and rinse with cool water.
2. Mix pasta, peppers, oranges, green onion, spinach, carrots and dressing in large bowl. Toss to coat well. Top with Chow Mein noodles. (For lunchboxes, pack Chow Mein noodles in a small container to be added right before eating to ensure optimal crunchiness!)
3. Serve with SunGold kiwi and edamame

PROTEIN BOX

🍴 2 servings

INGREDIENTS:

- 6-8 slices of deli turkey, rolled
- 2 hard-boiled eggs
- 2 cups baby carrots
- 1/4 cup almonds, optional
- 1/2 cup hummus

INSTRUCTIONS:

1. Divide the rolled turkey, hard-boiled eggs, veggies, and almonds into 2 lunch containers.
2. Fill 2 small lidded containers with hummus and pack with the bento lunches.

HUMMUS & OLIVE

🍴 2 servings

INGREDIENTS:

- 2 single-serve hummus containers
- 2 cheese sticks, cubed
- 1/3 cup pitted black olives
- 2 ounces turkey Pepperoni
- 1/2 cup roasted red bell pepper strips Pita chips

INSTRUCTIONS:

1. Divide the ingredients into 2 lunch containers with compartments.
2. Pack the pita chips into separate containers to prevent them from getting soggy.

FRUIT & CHEESE

2 servings

INGREDIENTS:

- 2-4 hard-boiled eggs, halved
- 2 ounces cheese cubes
- 1 cup baby carrots
- 2 apples, sliced
- Whole grain crackers

INSTRUCTIONS:

1. Divide the eggs, cheese, carrots, fruit, and apples into 2 lunch containers with compartments.
2. Pack the crackers in separate containers to prevent them from getting soggy.

HUMMUS, PITA & CHEESE

4 servings

INGREDIENTS:

- 2 pitas, sliced into wedges
- 1/4 cup feta cheese
- 1/2 medium cucumber, cubed
- 1/2 cup pitted olives
- 1/2 cup hummus or 2 single-serve cups

INSTRUCTIONS:

1. Divide the pita wedges, cheese, sliced cucumber, and olives into 2 lunch containers with compartments.
2. Pack the hummus into 2 lidded sauce containers and send it with the bento boxes.

FIESTA LUNCH

2 servings

INGREDIENTS:

- 2 packs of single-serve guacamole or 1/2 cup guacamole Tortilla chips
- 1/2 cup grape tomatoes
- 1 cup baby carrots
- 2 hard-boiled eggs
- 2 cups strawberries, halved

INSTRUCTIONS:

1. Evenly divide the ingredients into 2 lunch containers or compartmentalized lunch containers, making sure to keep the chips separate from the rest of the ingredients to prevent them from getting soggy.
2. If needed pack the guacamole in 2 lidded sauce containers and send it with the rest of the lunch.

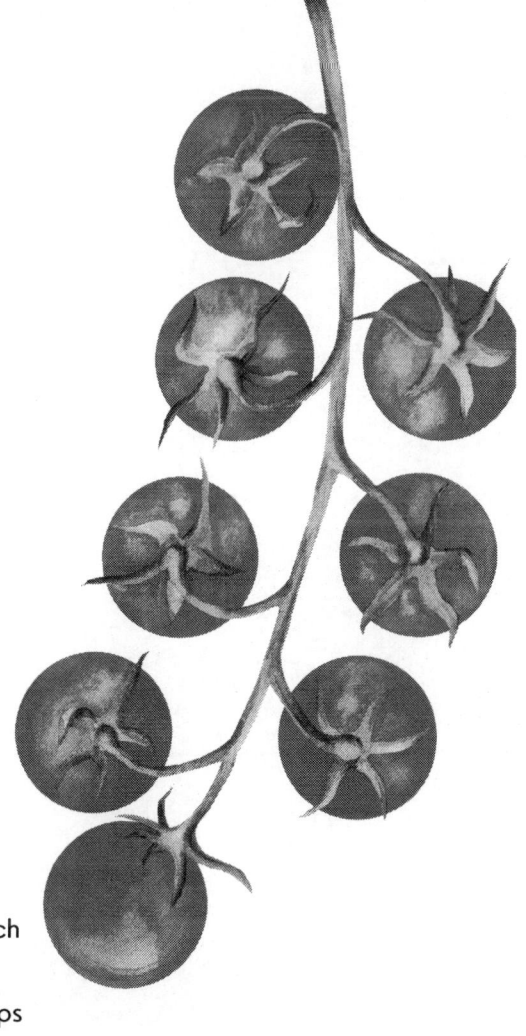

LOW CARB BOX

🍴 2 servings

INGREDIENTS:
- 2 hard-boiled eggs
- 6 slices of deli turkey, rolled
- 2 slices Provolone cheese, cut into squares 2 apples, sliced
- 1 cup baby carrots
- 1/2 cup hummus

INSTRUCTIONS:
1. In a lunch container with compartments, evenly divide the ingredients, making sure to keep the crackers separate from the fruit and veggies, to prevent them from getting soggy.
2. Divide the hummus between 2 lidded sauce containers and pack with the bento boxes.

VEGETABLE & HUMMUS BOX

🍴 2 servings

INGREDIENTS:
- 1 cup carrot sticks
- 1 cucumber, sliced
- 1 cup grape tomatoes 1/2 cup pitted olives 1/2 cup hummus
- 2 servings of cheese crisps

INSTRUCTIONS:
1. Evenly divide the ingredients into 2 lunch containers, making sure to keep the cheese crisps from the veggies.
2. Pack the hummus into 2 lidded sauce containers.

UN-SANDWICH BOX

🍴 2 servings

INGREDIENTS:

- 6 slices deli turkey, rolled up 1 cup grape tomatoes
- 1 cup carrot sticks
- 1 cucumber, sliced
- 2 servings of cheese crisp

INSTRUCTIONS:

1. Evenly divide the ingredients into 2 lunch containers, making sure to keep the cheese crisps from the veggies.

THE COBB BOX

🍴 2 servings

INGREDIENTS:

- 8-ounce grilled chicken breast fillet 1 cup sugar snap peas
- 1 cup grape tomatoes
- 2 slices bacon, halved
- 2 hard-boiled eggs
- 2 servings cheese crisps

INSTRUCTIONS:

1. Evenly divide the ingredients into 2 lunch containers, making sure to keep the cheese crisps from the veggies.

THE HOMEMADE LUNCHABLE

🍴 2 servings

INGREDIENTS:

- 2 slices Cheddar cheese, cut into 4 squares 8 slices deli meat, rolled
- 1/2 cup blueberries
- 1 cup strawberries, halved
- 2 rolls dried fruit Whole grain crackers

INSTRUCTIONS:

1. Evenly divide the ingredients into 2 lunch containers with compartments. Pack the crackers in separate containers to prevent them from getting soggy.

THE FRENCH WAY LUNCH

🍴 2 servings

INGREDIENTS:

- 3 ounces Brie cheese, sliced into 6 slices
- 2 cups grapes
- 1 apple sliced
- 1 cup baby carrots
- Whole grain crackers

INSTRUCTIONS:

1. Evenly divide the ingredients between 2 lunch containers with compartments. Make sure to keep the crackers separate from the rest of the ingredients.

PEANUT BUTTER & JELLY

2 servings

INGREDIENTS:

- 3 tablespoons peanut butter or nut-free alternative
- 4 slices of sandwich bread
- 2 tablespoons strawberry jam
- 1 cup baby carrots
- 1/2 cup blueberries 1 cup strawberries
- 1 apple, sliced

INSTRUCTIONS:

1. Spread the peanut butter over 2 slices and the jam over the remaining slices. Top 2 slices with the bananas and assemble the sandwiches.
2. Slice each PB & J into 4 quarters and divide into lunch containers along with the baby carrots and fruit.

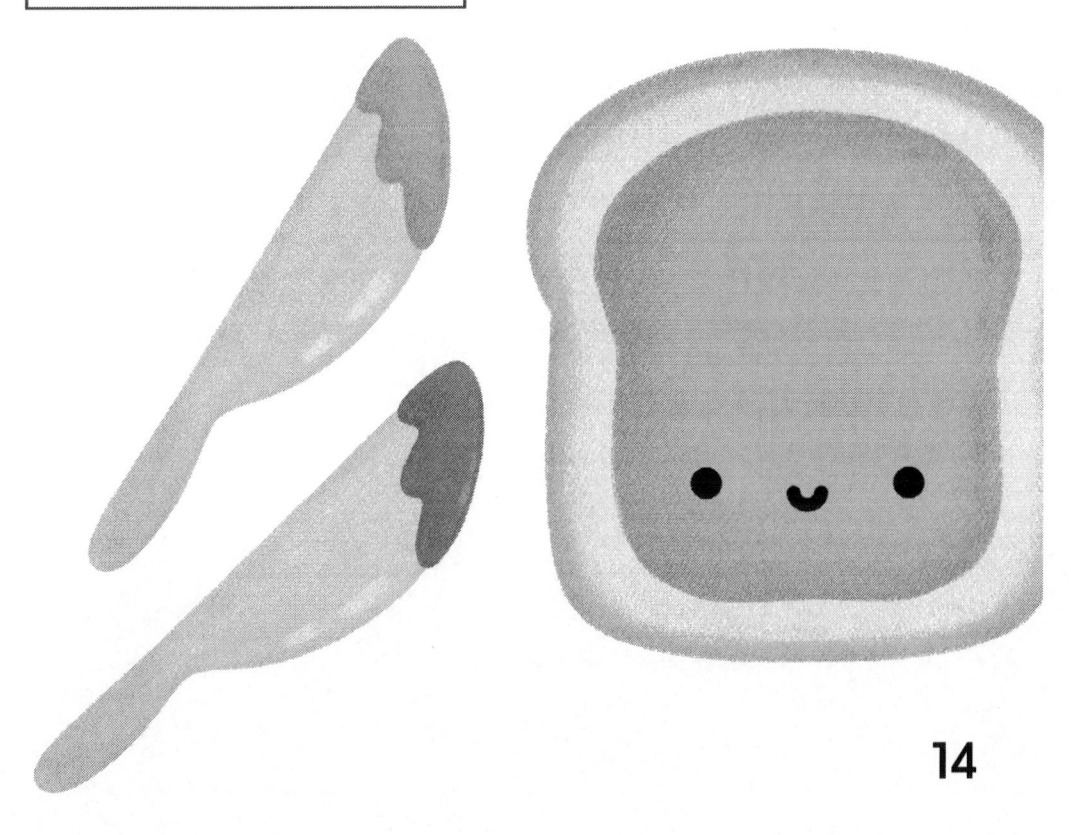

KOREAN BBQ CHICKPEA

2 servings

INGREDIENTS:

- 3 tablespoons tamari
- 2 tablespoons water
- 2 tablespoons tomato sauce
- 2 teaspoons honey or coconut sugar
- 1/4 teaspoon ground ginger
- 1/4 teaspoon pepper
- 1 teaspoon minced garlic
- 1 tablespoon sesame oil
- 2 to 3 tablespoons chopped green onion or red onion
- 1 can cooked chickpeas
- 1/2 cup unshelled cooked edamame, optional
- 2 cups cooked rice
- 1 cup chopped Brussels sprouts or shredded cabbage
- 1 zucchini, ribbon cut
- 1 carrot, ribbon cut
- 1 cup sliced grape tomatoes
- 1/2 lime, juiced
- 2 tablespoons sesame seeds
- 1/2 tablespoon crushed red pepper flakes
- Fine sea salt
- Pepper
- 1 cup of microgreens
- Handful of fresh cilantro

INSTRUCTIONS:

1. reheat the oven to 400 degrees F. Line a baking sheet with foil.
2. To make the Korean BBQ marinade, combine the tamari, water, tomato sauce, honey, ginger, pepper, garlic, sesame oil, and green onion in a medium-sized bowl. Add the chickpeas and edamame, if desired, to the marinade bowl and toss thoroughly to cover. Reserve 1 to 2 tablespoons (15 to 30 ml) of the marinade for topping the bowl.
3. Spread out the chickpea mixture on the prepared baking sheet. Roast for 15-20 minutes, turning once until the chickpeas are crispy. Remove from the oven and set aside. Let the chickpeas cool while preparing the bowls.
4. For the bowls, divide the cooked rice into 2 bowls, or 3 bowls for smaller portions. Top the rice bowls with Brussels sprouts, zucchini, carrot, and tomatoes, followed by the BBQ roasted chickpeas.
5. Squeeze the fresh lime juice on top of each bowl, then sprinkle with the sesame seeds and red pepper flakes. Season with salt or pepper, to taste, and garnish with the microgreens and fresh cilantro. For more BBQ zing, drizzle the reserved marinade sauce on top, or swap it out for your favorite BBQ sauce.

COLD LUNCHES

16

THE APPLE WRAP

🍴 2 servings

INGREDIENTS:
- 6-8 slices deli ham
- 3-4 slices Cheddar cheese, halved
- 2 apples, sliced into wedges

INSTRUCTIONS:
1. On a flat surface, place a ham slice. Top with half a slice of cheese and an apple wedge on top of the cheese. Using the ham, wrap the apple and the cheese. Repeat with remaining ham slices.
2. Place the wrapped apple slices inside 2 lunch containers along with remaining apple wedges. Pack with fruit and veggies.

ITALIAN PASTA SALAD

🍴 2 servings

INGREDIENTS:
- 2 cups cooked rotini pasta
- 1/2 cup halved grape tomatoes
- 1/3 cup sliced black olives
- 1/2 cup cubed Mozzarella cheese 1 tablespoon olive oil
- 1 tablespoon red wine vinegar Salt & black pepper, to taste

INSTRUCTIONS:
1. In a large bowl, combine the pasta, tomatoes, olives, cheese, olive oil, vinegar, salt, and black pepper. Toss to combine and divide between 2 lunch containers along with cheese.

LOUISIANA PASTA SALAD

4 servings

INGREDIENTS:

- 8 ounces Farfelle or Rotini pasta
- 1/2 cup mayonnaise or plain Greek yogurt 2 tablespoons Dijon or Creole mustard
- 1 teaspoon Creole seasoning
- 2 hard-boiled eggs, chopped
- 1/2 red bell pepper, diced
- 1 rib celery, diced
- 1/2 cup chopped red onion

INSTRUCTIONS:

1. Cook pasta according to package directions. Drain and rinse, allow to cool completely.
2. In a large bowl, whisk the mayonnaise, mustard, and seasoning until smooth. Add the cooled pasta, chopped eggs, bell pepper, celery, and red onion. Toss to combine, cover, and refrigerate 4 hours or overnight.
3. Divide the pasta salad into 4 lunch containers.

STUFFED AVOCADO

2-4 servings

INGREDIENTS:

- 4 hard-boiled eggs, diced small
- 1 tablespoon yellow mustard
- 3/4 teaspoon paprika
- 3 tablespoons mayo or plain Greek yogurt Pinch of salt
- Pinch of pepper
- Chives for garnish
- 2 avocados, halved and pitted

INSTRUCTIONS:

1. In a medium bowl, combine the diced eggs, mustard,
2. paprika, mayonnaise or yogurt, salt, and pepper.
3. Slice the avocado in half and remove the pit. With a spoon, stuff each avocado half the egg salad and serve or pack into lunch containers.

STRAWBERRY PARFAIT

2 servings

INGREDIENTS:
- 2 6-ounce vanilla Greek yogurts, or plain
- 2 tablespoons almond butter or nut-butter alternative
- 6 strawberries, sliced
- 1/2 cup granola or whole grain cereal

INSTRUCTIONS:
1. In a small bowl, mix the yogurt and almond butter.
2. Evenly divide the sliced strawberries between 2 thermos containers and top with the yogurt.
3. Divide the granola into 2 small containers or zip bags, and sprinkle on top of parfait prior to eating.

BLUEBERRY PARFAIT

2 ervings

INGREDIENTS:
- 1 cup of blueberries
- 2 cups vanilla Greek yogurt 1/2 cup granola

INSTRUCTIONS:
1. Divide the blueberries between 2 thermos containers, top with yogurt.
2. Divide the granola inside 2 small containers or zip bags and sprinkle on top of parfait prior to eating.

PEACH PARFAIT

🍴 2 servings

INGREDIENTS:

- 2 cups vanilla Greek yogurt
- 1 fresh peach, sliced
- 1/4 cup low sugar granola or whole grain cereal
- 4 graham cracker sheets

INSTRUCTIONS:

1. Divide the yogurt between 2 thermos or leak-proof containers.
2. Evenly divide the sliced peach, graham crackers, and granola into 2 lunch containers, keeping the granola and crackers separate from the fruit so they don't get soggy.

KITCHEN NOTE:
Don't have fresh peaches? Use 1 cup frozen peach slices.

ANTIPASTO PASTA SALAD

2 servings

INGREDIENTS:

- 1 cup mini conchiglie rigate, cooked and tossed with olive oil so they don't stick together
- 2 ounces salami
- 2 ounces pepperoni
- 2 ounces pepperoncini
- 2 ounces cucumber slices
- 2 ounces roasted red peppers
- 2 ounces red onion, chopped
- 2 ounces green olives
- 2 ounces black olives
- 2 ounces grape tomatoes
- 2 ounces artichoke hearts
- 2 ounces fresh red pepper
- 2 ounces Italian dressing

INSTRUCTIONS:

1. Combine all ingredients and divide into 2.
2. Place in lunchbox container

GREEK PASTA SALAD

🍴 2 servings

INGREDIENTS:

- 1 cup rotini pasta, cooked and tossed with olive oil to keep it from sticking
- 2 ounces green olives, pimento stuffed
- 2 ounces feta cheese crumbles
- 2 ounces cucumbers, diced
- 2 ounces red onion
- 2 ounces grape tomatoes
- 2 ounces Tzatziki ranch dressing

INSTRUCTIONS:

1. Combine all ingredients, minus dressing, and divide into 2.
2. Place in lunchbox container. Serve with dressing on the side.

BBQ CHICKEN PASTA SALAD

2 servings

INGREDIENTS:

- 1 cup bowtie pasta, cooked and tossed with olive oil to keep it from sticking
- 4 ounces rotisserie chicken breasts, chunked
- 2 ounces green onions, sliced
- 2 ounces of black beans
- 2 ounces whole kernel corn
- 2 ounces cheddar cheese chunks
- 2 ounces ranch dressing mixed with BBQ sauce

INSTRUCTIONS:

1. Combine all ingredients, minus dressing, and divide into 2.
2. Place in lunchbox container. Serve with dressing on the side.

RASPBERRY CHICKEN PASTA SALAD

2 servings

INGREDIENTS:

- 1 cup mini conchiglie rigate, cooked and tossed with olive oil so they don't stick together
- 2 ounces carrots, chunked
- 2 ounces broccoli, chunked
- 4 ounces rotisserie chicken breast chunks
- 2 ounces raspberry vinaigrette dressing

INSTRUCTIONS:

1. Combine all ingredients, minus dressing, and divide into 2.
2. Place in lunchbox container. Serve with dressing on the side.

CAESAR PASTA SALAD

2 servings

INGREDIENTS:

- 1 cup bowtie pasta, cooked and tossed with olive oil so they don't stick together
- 2 ounces parmesan cheese
- 1 cup romaine lettuce, washed and chopped
- 4 ounces rotisserie chicken breast chunks
- 2 ounces caesar dressing

INSTRUCTIONS:

1. Combine all ingredients, minus dressing, and divide into 2.
2. Place in lunchbox container. Serve with dressing on the side.

RAINBOW PASTA SALAD

🍴 2 servings

INGREDIENTS:

- 1 cup bowtie pasta, cooked and tossed with olive oil to keep it from sticking
- 2 ounces pepperoni, chunked
- 2 ounces cucumbers, chunked
- 2 ounces carrots, chunked
- 2 ounces broccoli, chunked
- 2 ounces cheddar cheese chunks
- 2 ounces black olives
- 2 ounces grape tomatoes
- 2 ounces red pepper, diced
- 2 ounces yellow pepper, diced
- 2 ounces red onion, diced
- 2 ounces ranch dressing

INSTRUCTIONS:

1. Combine all ingredients, minus dressing, and divide into 2.
2. Place in lunchbox container. Serve with dressing on the side.

PIZZA PASTA SALAD

2 servings

INGREDIENTS:

- 1 cup rotini pasta, cooked and tossed with olive oil to keep it from sticking.
- 2 ounces black olives,
- 2 ounces cheddar cheese chunks
- 2 ounces pepperoni, chunked
- 2 ounces grape tomatoes
- 2 ounces Italian dressing

INSTRUCTIONS:

1. Combine all ingredients, minus dressing, and divide into 2.
2. Place in lunchbox container. Serve with dressing on the side.

SEVEN LAYER DIP

2 servings

INGREDIENTS:

- 1/2 cup hummus
- 2 tablespoons crumbled feta cheese 1/4 cup sliced black olives
- 1/4 cup halved grape tomatoes
- 1/4 teaspoon dried oregano

INSTRUCTIONS:

1. Divide the hummus between 2 8-ounce lunch containers. Spread it over the bottom of the containers and top with feta, olives, tomato, and oregano.
2. Pack the dip cups with crackers, veggies, and fruit.

DELI ROLL-UPS

2 ervings

INGREDIENTS:

- 6 slices of deli turkey
- 3 slices Cheddar cheese, halved 1 cup strawberries
- 1/2 cup blueberries
- Whole grain crackers

INSTRUCTIONS:

1. Divide the blueberries between
2. Place the deli turkey onto a cutting board, and top each turkey slice with cheese. Roll and repeat with remaining turkey and cheese slices. Evenly divide the rolls ups between 2 lunch containers along with the fruit.
3. Make sure to keep the crackers separate from the rest of the ingredients.

TOMATO PASTA SALAD

2 servings

INGREDIENTS:

- 2 cups cooked macaroni or Penne pasta 1/2-pint grape tomatoes, halved
- 1 tablespoon olive oil
- 1 teaspoon dried basil
- 1/2 teaspoon salt
- 1/4 teaspoon black pepper

INSTRUCTIONS:

1. In a large bowl combine the macaroni, tomatoes, olive oil, basil, salt and pepper.
2. Toss to combine and divide the pasta salad inside 2 lunch containers.

HOT LUNCHES

BASIC NUTRITION
estd. 2020
EAT REAL FOOD

SLOW COOKER MINESTRONE

6 servings

INGREDIENTS:

- 1 yellow onion, diced
- 3 carrots, peeled and sliced
- 28-ounce can of diced tomatoes, drained and rinsed
- 2 tablespoons tomato paste
- 4 cups vegetable broth
- 2 cups of water
- 1 tablespoon Italian seasoning
- 1 teaspoon garlic powder
- 1 teaspoon salt
- 1/2 teaspoon black pepper
- 8 ounces shelled pasta
- 2 15-ounce cans of cannellini beans, drained and rinsed 1 zucchini, sliced
- 15-ounce can green beans, drained and rinsed 1/3 cup shredded Parmesan

INSTRUCTIONS:

1. Add the onion, garlic, carrots, tomatoes, tomato paste, broth, and water to a slow-cooker dish. Season with Italian seasoning, garlic powder, salt, and pepper. Stir to combine, cover with a lid and cook for 6 to 8 hours on low or 3 to 4 hours on high.
2. 30 minutes prior to serving, add the pasta, zucchini, beans, and green beans. Cook on high heat for 25 to 30 minutes, until the pasta is tender and the soup has thickened.
3. Ladle soup into thermos containers, top with cheese, and seal.

KITCHEN NOTE:
Swap the cannellini beans for your favorite variety of beans.

ENCHILADA SOUP

6 servings

INGREDIENTS:

- 3 tablespoons olive oil
- 2 garlic cloves, minced
- 1 medium onion, chopped
- 3 tablespoons chili powder
- 1 teaspoon dried oregano
- 1 teaspoon cumin
- 1/2 teaspoon salt
- 1/2 teaspoon smoked paprika
- 4 cups vegetable or chicken broth 2–15 ounce cans of pinto beans, rinsed and drained
- 12-ounce bag of frozen corn, thawed 28-ounce can of fire-roasted tomatoes

INSTRUCTIONS:

1. In a large 5-quart pot, heat oil over medium-high
2. heat.
3. Add the chopped onion and garlic; sauté until the onion is
4. tender and translucent.
5. Season with chili powder, oregano, cumin, salt, and
6. paprika. Cook for 3 minutes or until fragrant. Next, add
7. in broth, pinto beans, corn, and crushed tomatoes.
8. Bring soup to a boil and reduce heat to a simmer; cook for 20 minutes, stirring a few times to combine.
9. Ladle the soup into thermos containers and seal.

POTATO SOUP

8 servings

INGREDIENTS:

- 1 onion, chopped
- 1-pound yellow potatoes, peeled and cut into 1 1/2-inch cube
- 8 oz ham steak, cubed
- 32-ounce carton of chicken or vegetable broth
- 2 cups whole milk
- 1/2 teaspoon pepper
- Shredded Cheddar cheese
- 6 slices of bacon, cooked and chopped
- 4 green onions, chopped

INSTRUCTIONS:

1. In the bowl of a 6-quart slow cooker, combine the onions, potatoes, ham, broth, milk, and black pepper. Cover and cook on low for 6 hours.
2. Once the soup is cooked and potatoes are tender, use the back of a large spoon to mash some of the potato pieces. Stir to combine.
3. Divide the soup into thermos containers. Top with cheese, bacon, and chopped green onions. Seal and pack.

KITCHEN NOTE:

Make this recipe dairy-free and omit the milk. Add 2 cups additional chicken broth. Refrigerate leftovers for up to 3 days.

GRILLED CHEESE & TOMATO BASIL SOUP

8 servings

INGREDIENTS:

- 1 tablespoon olive oil
- 1 red bell pepper, diced
- 2 medium carrots, diced
- 1 zucchini, diced
- 1 rib celery, diced
- 1 small onion, diced
- 2 cloves garlic, minced
- 2 tablespoons tomato paste
- 2 28-ounce cans of crushed tomatoes or puréed tomatoes
- Fresh Basil Leaves
- 2 cups vegetable stock
- 4 grilled cheese sandwiches, cut into strips

INSTRUCTIONS:

1. Add all ingredients inside a slow cooker. Cook for 6 hours on low.
2. Once the soup is cooked down, insert an immersion blender and blend until smooth.
3. Prior to serving, prepare the grilled cheese sandwiches and slice into strips. Divide the 4 servings of soup into 4 thermos containers and pack with the grilled cheese strips.

KITCHEN NOTE:
Refrigerate the remaining soup in an airtight container for up to 4 days.

CHICKEN TERIYAKI

4 servings

INGREDIENTS:

- 1 1/2 pounds boneless, skinless chicken breasts or thighs
- 1/4 cup brown sugar, honey, or coconut palm sugar
- 1/2 cup coconut aminos or low-sodium soy sauce
- 1/4 cup of water
- 1 small garlic clove, grated
- 1 teaspoon grated fresh ginger 1 tablespoon oil
- 3 cups cooked rice
- Green onions, chopped

INSTRUCTIONS:

1. Pound the chicken breasts or thighs to 1/4- inch thickness.
2. In a medium bowl, whisk the brown sugar, coconut aminos, water, grated garlic, and ginger until combined. Place the chicken inside a large zip bag and add the sauce. Seal and shake to combine. Marinade the chicken for 30 minutes or overnight for more flavor.
3. In a large skillet, heat the oil over medium heat. Add the chicken and cook for 3 minutes on each side or until browned; remove from the skillet. Repeat the process with the remaining chicken, if necessary.
4. Once the chicken is cooked, pour the contents of the zip bag into the empty skillet. Bring the sauce to a boil, then reduce heat to medium-low and simmer for 2 minutes or until thickened.
5. Bring the chicken back to the skillet and toss to combine with the sauce. Remove from heat.
6. Scoop the rice into thermos containers and top with the teriyaki chicken and green onions. Top with lid and seal.

BUFFALO SWEET POTATOES

4 servings

INGREDIENTS:

- 1 pound boneless, skinless chicken breasts
- 1 cup Buffalo sauce
- 4 medium sweet potatoes, baked
- Blue cheese crumbles, optional 2 green onions, sliced
- 1/4 - 1/2 cup ranch dressing

INSTRUCTIONS:

1. Place the chicken in the dish of a slow cooker, top with Buffalo sauce and toss to coat. Cover and set on low for 8 hours or high for 5 hours.
2. Once the chicken is cooked through and easily shreds apart between 2 forks shred the meat in the slow cooker dish and toss to coat with the sauce.
3. Meanwhile, cook each medium potato in the microwave for about 6 minutes, flipping it half-way through or, bake the potatoes in the oven at 375F for about 1 hour, until the meat feels tender when poked with a fork.
4. Slice each baked sweet potato, lengthwise. Open and use a fork to separate the sweet potato meat from the skin.
5. Top each potato with 1/2 cup buffalo chicken, Blue cheese crumbles, and green onions. Pack each potato into a thermos container and seal. Divide the ranch dressing between 4 lidded sauce containers and send with the Buffalo Chicken Potatoes.

PESTO PASTA

2 servings

INGREDIENTS:

- 2 cups cooked macaroni pasta
- 2 tablespoons pesto sauce
- 1/2 cup grape tomatoes

INSTRUCTIONS:

1. In a large bowl, combine the pasta, pesto sauce, and grape tomatoes.
2. Toss to combine and divide between 2 thermos or lunch containers.

CHEESY RICE FRITTERS

2 servings

INGREDIENTS:

- 1 cup brown rice
- 3/4 cup grated cheese
- 3 eggs, lightly beaten
- 1 medium carrot, peeled and grated
- 1 small zucchini, grated
- 1 tsp dried basil
- 1/4 cup plain flour
- Salt and pepper
- Olive oil to shallow fry
- 1 cup grape tomatoes, halved lengthways
- Bunch of watercress

INSTRUCTIONS:

1. In a large mixing bowl mix together the rice, cheese, eggs, carrot, zucchini, basil, and flour. Season well with salt and pepper.
2. Heat the olive oil in a large fry pan over moderately high heat. Fill a 1/4 cup measure with the mixture and turn into the hot pan, flatten into a round fritter shape, and continue shaping the mixture to fill the pan. Cook the fritters in batches for 2-3 minutes on each side or until golden brown and crisp. Transfer the cooked fritters to a plate lined with a paper towel.
3. Serve the fritters warm or cool tumbled with the grape tomatoes and watercress.

BOWLS

· BASIC ·
estd. 2020
NUTRITION
EAT REAL FOOD

THAI CHICKEN BOWL

4 servings

INGREDIENTS:

Thai Chicken Bowls:
- 2 tablespoons oil
- 2 tablespoons soy sauce
- 1 tablespoon Sriracha sauce
- 1 lb boneless, skinless chicken breasts 3 cups cooked Jasmine rice
- 16-ounce bag shredded cabbage
- 2 medium carrots, shredded
- 1/4 cup chopped cilantro
- 2 tablespoons chopped peanuts, optional

Peanut Sauce:
- 1/3 cup creamy peanut butter*
- 2 tablespoons honey
- 1 tablespoon fresh lime juice
- 1 tablespoon soy sauce or coconut aminos 1 clove garlic, grated
- 1 teaspoon Sriracha sauce
- 1–2 tablespoons hot water

INSTRUCTIONS:

1. Preheat the at 425F. Line a baking sheet with parchment paper.
2. In a large bowl, whisk the oil with the soy sauce and Sriracha. Add the chicken breasts and toss to combine. Cover with plastic wrap and refrigerate for 30 minutes or overnight for extra flavor.
3. Bake the chicken for 20 minutes or until the internal temperature reaches 165F. Remove the chicken and allow to rest for 5 minutes prior to slicing.
4. In a medium bowl, combine the peanut butter, honey, lime juice, soy sauce, garlic, and Sriracha sauce. Add one tablespoon of water and whisk to combine. Add additional hot water until the Peanut Sauce reaches the desired consistency.
5. Divide the cooked rice into 4 lunch containers, and top with sliced chicken, cabbage, carrots, cilantro, and peanuts, if used. Drizzle with Peanut Sauce.

THAI PASTA

🍴 2 servings

INGREDIENTS:

Peanut Sauce:
- 1/3 cup creamy peanut butter
- 2 tablespoons honey
- 1 tablespoon fresh lime juice
- 1 tablespoon soy sauce or coconut aminos
- 1 clove garlic, grated
- 1 teaspoon Sriracha sauce
- 1–2 tablespoons hot water

Thai Chicken Pasta:
- 2 cups cooked Penne pasta
- 2 chicken breasts, sliced
- 1 cup shredded carrots
- 1 cup shredded purple cabbage 1 red bell pepper, sliced Peanut Sauce or sesame ginger dressing
- 2 cups cubed pineapple

INSTRUCTIONS:

1. In a medium bowl, combine the peanut butter, honey, lime juice, soy sauce, garlic, and Sriracha sauce. Add one tablespoon of water and whisk to combine. Add additional hot water until the Peanut Sauce reaches the desired consistency. Refrigerate in an airtight container for up to 2 weeks.
2. Divide the cooked pasta between 2 lunch containers. Top with chicken, carrots, cabbage, bell pepper, and a drizzle of the Peanut Sauce or salad dressing. Pack with the fruit.

KOREAN CHICKEN BOWL

🍴 4 servings

INGREDIENTS:

- 3 tablespoons soy sauce or coconut aminos 2 tablespoons brown sugar or honey
- 2 tablespoons sesame oil
- 1 tablespoon Sriracha sauce
- 2 garlic cloves, minced
- 1 teaspoon ground ginger
- 1 lb boneless, skinless chicken breasts 3 cups cooked Jasmine rice

Cabbage Slaw
- 2 tablespoons of rice wine vinegar
- 1 tablespoon honey
- 1 tablespoon sesame oil
- 16-ounce bag coleslaw mix
- 1 red bell pepper, thinly sliced 1/4 cup chopped cilantro

INSTRUCTIONS:

1. In a medium bowl, whisk the soy sauce with the honey, sesame oil, Sriracha sauce, garlic, and ginger. Transfer the mixture to a large zip bag or airtight container and add the chicken breasts. Seal and marinate for 30 minutes to 4 hours.
2. Preheat the at 425F. Line a baking sheet with parchment paper.
3. Place the chicken breasts onto the baking sheet and bake for 20 minutes or until the chicken reaches an internal temperature of 165F.
4. Meanwhile, prepare the slaw. In a large bowl, whisk the rice wine vinegar with the honey and sesame oil. Add the coleslaw mix or slaw mix, and chopped cilantro, toss to combine.
5. Once the chicken is cooked through, remove from the oven and allow to rest for 5 minutes before slicing.
6. Divide the cooked rice into 4 lunch containers, top with sliced chicken and cabbage slaw.

MEDITERRANEAN BOWL

4 servings

INGREDIENTS:

- 1 cup farro
- 3 cups water or stock
- 1/2 teaspoon salt
- 2 grilled chicken breasts, sliced
- 1 pint cherry tomatoes, halved
- 2 cups chopped cucumber
- 1 cup kalamata olives, pitted and sliced 1/2 red onion, sliced
- 1 cup tzatziki sauce
- 1/2 cup crumbled feta cheese

INSTRUCTIONS:

1. Rinse and drain farro. Place farro in a pot with salt and enough water or stock to cover it. Bring it to a boil; reduce heat to medium-low and simmer for 30 minutes. Drain off any excess water.
2. To assemble the Greek bowls; place a bed of farro at the bottom of your bowl or meal prep container. Top with sliced chicken, tomatoes, cucumber, olives, red onion, tzatziki sauce, and feta cheese.

CHICKEN BUFFALO BOWL

4 servings

INGREDIENTS:

- 1-pound boneless, skinless chicken breasts 1 cup Buffalo sauce
- 3 cups cooked rice, warm
- 1 avocado, peeled, pitted, and diced
- 1 cup grape tomatoes, halved 1/4 cup crumbled blue cheese
- 1/2 cup ranch dressing

INSTRUCTIONS:

1. Place the chicken breasts into the dish of a slow cooker. Pour the buffalo sauce over the chicken and stir to combine. Cover and cook on low for 7 to 8 hours or high for 4 to 5 hours.
2. Once the chicken is cooked through, shred the meat with 2 forks and toss to coat with the sauce.
3. Divide the cooked rice between 4 thermos or lunch containers and top with Buffalo chicken, avocado, tomatoes, and blue cheese crumbles.
4. Divide the Ranch dressing inside 4 lidded sauce containers and pack with the Buffalo Chicken Bowls.

PEA AND NOODLE FRITTERS

4-6 servings

INGREDIENTS:

- 1 1/4 cups frozen peas
- 1/2 x 440g packet shelf-fresh Hokkien noodles
- 1/4 cup flour
- 1/4 cup milk
- 2 eggs, lightly beaten
- 1/4 cup grated parmesan
- 1 red onion, finely chopped
- 1/4 cup rice bran oil
- Cherry tomatoes, to serve
- Carrot sticks, to serve
- Celery sticks, to serve

INSTRUCTIONS:

1. Place peas in a heatproof bowl. Cover with boiling water. Stand for 2 minutes or until bright green and tender. Drain. Refresh under cold water. Return to bowl. Roughly mash peas with a fork. Add noodles, flour, milk, eggs, parmesan, and onion. Season with salt and pepper. Stir to combine.

2. Heat oil in a large frying pan over medium heat. Drop 1/4 cup batter into the pan, spreading to form a circle. Repeat to make 4 fritters. Cook for 2 minutes or until golden underneath. Turn. Cook for 2 minutes or until cooked through. Transfer to a plate lined with a paper towel to drain. Repeat with the remaining batter. Serve with cherry tomatoes and carrot and celery sticks.

BURRITO BOWL

🍴 2 servings

INGREDIENTS:

- 1 cup black beans
- 1/2 cup frozen corn, thawed
- 1/2 teaspoon salt
- 1/4 teaspoon black pepper
- 1 1/2 cups cooked rice
- 1/4 cup shredded Cheddar cheese
- 1/2 cup salsa
- 2 single-serve guacamole packs or 1/4 cup guacamole

INSTRUCTIONS:

1. In a medium, microwave-safe bowl, combine the black beans and corn. Season with salt and black pepper. Microwave on high, for 1 minute or until heated through.
2. Divide the rice between 2 thermos or lunch containers, and top with black beans and corn, cheese, and salsa. Seal the containers and pack with guacamole cups.

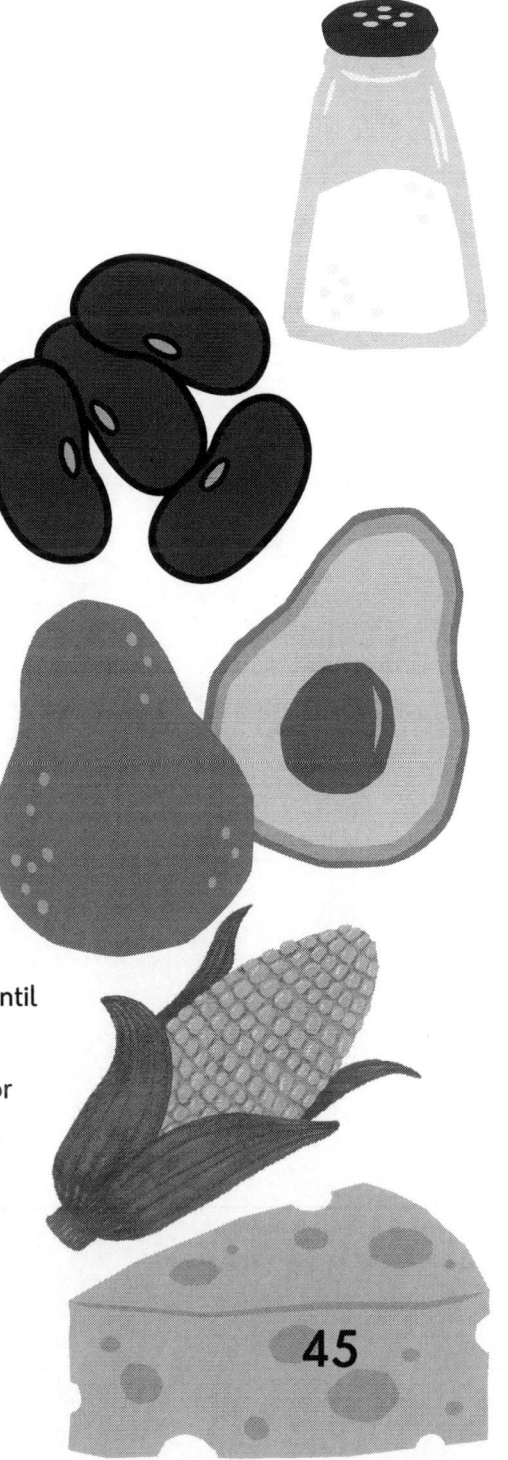

SALADS

ASIAN KALE SALAD

4 servings

INGREDIENTS:

Sesame Ginger Dressing:
- 1/2 cup rice vinegar
- 1/4 cup soy sauce
- 3 tablespoons sesame seeds
- 1 tablespoons brown sugar
- 2 teaspoons fresh ginger, grated 1 garlic clove, grated
- 1 1/2 teaspoons sesame oil

Asian Kale Salad:
- 4 cups chopped kale
- 1 cup red cabbage, shredded
- 1/2 cup shredded carrots
- 1 cup shelled edamame, thawed if using frozen 1/2 cup thinly sliced red onion 1/4 cup sunflower seeds

INSTRUCTIONS:

1. In a lidded jar, combine the dressing ingredients. Top with lid, seal, and shake to combine. Refrigerate for up to 1 week.
2. In a large bowl, combine the kale, cabbage, carrots, edamame, red onion, and sunflower seeds. Toss to combine.
3. Divide the salad into 4 lunch
4. containers.
5. Divide 2 tablespoons of dressing each into 4 lidded sauce containers. Pack the dressing with the salads.

SALMON SALAD

🍴 4 servings

INGREDIENTS:

- 4 cups salad spring mix or chopped lettuce
- 1 cup frozen green beans, steamed
- 6-ounce can salmon in water, drained
- 1/2 cup grape tomatoes, halved
- 1/4 cup black or Kalamata olives
- 2 hard-boiled eggs, halved
- 1/4 cup vinaigrette dressing

INSTRUCTIONS:

1. Divide the salad greens into 2 lunch containers, top with green beans, salmon, tomatoes, olives, and eggs.
2. Pack the vinaigrette into 2 lidded sauce containers and send with the salads.

ANTIPASTA SALAD

🍴 2 servings

INGREDIENTS:
- 1/2 avocado, peeled and diced
- 6 slices deli turkey, rolled and sliced 1/2 cup grape tomatoes
- 2 slices Provolone cheese, cubed 1/4 cup pitted black olives
- 1 tablespoon basil pesto
- 2 oranges

INSTRUCTIONS:

1. Divide the avocado, turkey, tomatoes, cheese, and olives into 2 lunch containers making alternate rows of each.
2. Pack the pesto into lidded sauce containers and send with the salads.
3. Prior to serving, drizzle the pesto over the salad and toss to combine.

SANTA FE SALAD

2 servings

INGREDIENTS:

- 1/2 head Iceberg lettuce, chopped
- 8-ounce cooked chicken breasts, cubed
- 1/2 cup canned black beans, drained and rinsed 1/2 cup corn, thawed, if using frozen
- 1/2-pint grape tomatoes
- 1/4 cup shredded Cheddar cheese
- 1/2 avocado, peeled and diced
- 1/4 cup ranch dressing

INSTRUCTIONS:

1. Divide the Iceberg lettuce into 2 lunch containers, and top with chicken, black beans, corn, tomatoes, cheese, and avocado. Top with lid.
2. Divide the ranch dressing into 2 lidded sauce containers and pack with the salads.

COBB PASTA SALAD

🍴 4 servings

INGREDIENTS:

- 4 cups cooked macaroni
- 1/2 cup halved grape tomatoes
- 3 slices bacon, cooked and finely chopped
- 6 slices of turkey, chopped
- 2 hard-boiled eggs, chopped
- 1/4 cup shredded Cheddar cheese 1/4 cup ranch dressing

INSTRUCTIONS:

1. In a large bowl, combine the macaroni, grape tomatoes, bacon, turkey, egg, and cheese. Add the ranch dressing and toss to combine.
2. Divide the pasta into 4 lunch containers.

SALAD OF THE SOUTH

4-6 servings

INGREDIENTS:

- 2 tablespoons lemon juice
  1/2 cup mayonnaise
- 1/2 teaspoon salt
- 1/4 teaspoon black pepper 1 teaspoon cumin
- 3-4 cups shredded rotisserie chicken
- 1/2 cup chopped celery
- 3-4 cups mixed salad greens 1/2 cup halved grape tomatoes

INSTRUCTIONS:

1. In a large bowl, combine the lemon juice, mayonnaise, salt, pepper, and cumin, whisk until thoroughly combined. Add the chicken and fold with a spatula, add the celery and fold again until all the ingredients are fully combined.
2. Divide the salad greens between 2 lunch containers. Top each bed of lettuce with 3/4 cup chicken salad and grape tomatoes.

CORN & BLACK BEAN SALAD

2 servings

INGREDIENTS:

- 1 cup frozen corn, thawed
- 15-ounce can black beans, rinsed and drained 1/2-pint halved grape tomatoes, if available 1/4 teaspoon cumin
- 1/4 teaspoon salt
- 1/2 tablespoon olive oil
- 1/2 lime, juiced
- Tortilla chips, for serving

INSTRUCTIONS:

1. In a large bowl, combine the corn, black beans, grape tomatoes, cumin, salt, olive oil, and lime juice. Toss to combine.
2. Divide the salad between 2 lunch containers. Pack with tortilla chips.

SALAD BLT

2 servings

INGREDIENTS:

- 4 cups shredded Iceberg lettuce
- 1/2-pint cherry tomatoes, halved
- 1/2 cup shredded Mozzarella cheese
- 4 slices bacon, cooked and chopped 1/2 avocado, peeled and diced
- 1/4 cup ranch dressing

INSTRUCTIONS:

1. Divide the lettuce between 2 lunch containers. Top with tomatoes, cheese, bacon, and avocado.
2. Divide the ranch dressing between 2 lidded sauce containers. Pack with the salads.

FALAFEL SALAD

4 servings

INGREDIENTS:

Falafels:
- 2 cups canned chickpeas, drained and rinsed 1 tablespoon ground cumin
- 1 teaspoon coriander, optional
- 3 garlic cloves, minced
- 1/2 cup diced white onion
- 3 tablespoons freshly squeezed lemon juice 1/3 cup breadcrumbs
- 3 tablespoons olive oil, to pan-fry

Falafel Salads:
- 4 cups chopped Romaine lettuce 1/2-pint grape tomatoes, halved 1/2 cucumber, sliced
- 1/4 cup feta cheese crumbles Favorite vinaigrette

INSTRUCTIONS:

1. In a food processor or blender, combine the
2. chickpeas with the seasonings, garlic, onions, lemon juice, and breadcrumbs. Process until it becomes a smooth thick paste.
3. With wet hands, form dough into small balls, the size of a large walnut. Press down to form 1 1/2-inch patties. If the mixture is too sticky, add a little bit more breadcrumbs. If it's too dry, add a tablespoon or 2 of water.
4. In a large skillet, heat the oil over medium-high heat. Pan-fry the falafels for 3-4 minutes each side, or until sides are golden brown.
5. Remove falafel onto a paper towel-lined plate and blot excess oil with additional paper towels.
6. Divide the lettuce between 4 lunch containers. Top with the tomatoes, cucumber, cooked falafels, and feta cheese.
7. Divide the vinaigrette between 2 lidded sauce containers and pack with the salads.

FRIED RICE SALAD

4 servings

INGREDIENTS:

- 1 tbsp sesame oil
- 1 onion, finely chopped
- 1 red capsicum, seeded, finely chopped
- 1 green capsicum, seeded, finely chopped
- 2 rashers shortcut rindless bacon, finely chopped
- 4 cups cooked brown rice
- 125g can corn kernels, drained
- 6 green onions (shallots), thinly sliced
- 1/4 cup light soy sauce
- 1/4 cup hoisin sauce
- Cherry tomatoes, halved, to serve
- Coriander, leaves, to serve

INSTRUCTIONS:

1. Heat oil in a large frying pan or wok over high heat. Sauté onion, capsicum and bacon for 3-4 minutes.
2. Add rice, corn, green onions and sauces. Stir-fry for 2-3 minutes, mixing well. Transfer to a bowl to cool.
3. Spoon salad into lunchbox or other sealable container. Top with halved cherry tomatoes and coriander leaves. Keep chilled.

SWEET POTATO SALAD

2 servings

INGREDIENTS:

- 1/4 cup mayonnaise
- 1/4 teaspoon black pepper
- 1 teaspoon paprika
- 1/4 teaspoon thyme
- 2 medium baked sweet potatoes, peeled and diced
- 2 tablespoons diced red onion
- 2 tablespoons sliced green onions 1 rib chopped celery
- 2 hard-boiled eggs, peeled and sliced
- 1 green onion, diced

INSTRUCTIONS:

1. In a large bowl, combine the mayonnaise, black pepper, paprika, thyme and stir to combine.
2. Add the sweet potatoes, red onion, green onions, celery, and hard-boiled eggs. Toss to combine and sprinkle with additional green onions.
3. Divide the sweet potato salad into 2 lunch containers. Pack with fruit and veggies.

ROASTED VEGGIES & CHICKEN SALAD

4 servings

INGREDIENTS:

Chicken Marinade:

- 1/3 cup olive oil,
- 1 orange, zested
- 1 orange, juiced
- 1 teaspoon salt
- 1 1/2 pounds boneless skinless chicken breasts

Fall Vegetable Salad:

- 16-ounce bag butternut squash cubes
- 16-ounce bag Brussels sprouts, halved
- 2 medium beets, peeled and cubed
- 2 tablespoons olive oil
- 1 teaspoon salt
- 1/2 teaspoon garlic powder
- 6 cups spring salad mix or shredded lettuce Balsamic vinaigrette

INSTRUCTIONS:

1. Place marinade ingredients and chicken in a zip bag or airtight container and marinate for 20 minutes or up to 4 hours. Place one oven rack on the middle shelf and another directly below it. Preheat the oven to 375F. Line 2 baking sheets with parchment paper. Place the chicken breasts onto 1 baking sheet.
2. On the other baking sheet, make alternate rows of the butternut squash, Brussels sprouts, and beets. Drizzle the veggies with olive oil and season with salt and garlic powder. Toss the veggies to combine, keeping them in separate rows (if you combine all of them the beets will change the color of the other veggies).
3. Place the chicken on the top rack of the oven and the veggies directly beneath. Bake for 35-40 minutes, until the chicken is cooked to 165F and the veggies are tender (depending on the size of your cubed veggies, they might need to come out sooner).
4. Allow the chicken and vegetables to cool down to room temperature before slicing the chicken and assembling the meal prep. To pack for lunch, create a bed of lettuce into 4 meal prep containers, top with sliced chicken and roasted veggies.
5. Divide the balsamic dressing into 4 lidded sauce containers and pack with the salads.

CAPRESE SALAD WITH CHICKEN

2 servings

INGREDIENTS:

- 1 heart of Romaine lettuce, chopped
- 8-ounce cooked chicken breast, sliced
- 1/2 avocado, peeled, pitted, and diced
- 1/2 cup grape tomatoes, halved
- 1/4 cup shredded Mozzarella cheese
- 1/4 cup black olives
- 1/4 cup sliced basil leaves
- 1/4 cup balsamic vinaigrette

INSTRUCTIONS:

1. Divide the lettuce between 2 lunch containers. Top with chicken, avocado, grape tomatoes, Mozzarella cheese, black olives, and basil.
2. Divide the dressing into 2 lidded sauce containers and pack with salads.

COBB SALAD

🍴 2 servings

INGREDIENTS:
- 1/2 head Iceberg lettuce, chopped 2 hard-boiled eggs, sliced
- 4 slices deli ham, chopped
- 4 slices deli turkey, chopped
- 2 slices bacon, chopped
- 1/2 cup shredded Cheddar cheese
- 1/2 cup halved grape tomatoes
- 1/2 avocado, peeled, pitted, and diced
- 1/4 cup ranch dressing
- 2 cups strawberries

INSTRUCTIONS:
1. Divide the lettuce between 2 lunch containers. Top with egg, ham, turkey, bacon, cheese, grape tomatoes, and avocado.
2. Divide the Ranch dressing between 2 lidded sauce containers and pack with the fruit.

SANDWICHES, WRAPS, & MORE

COBB WRAP

2 servings

INGREDIENTS:

- 1 cup shredded lettuce
- 2 tablespoons ranch dressing
- 2 hard-boiled eggs, chopped
- 2 slices bacon, cooked crisp and crumbled 4 slices deli turkey, cut into bite-size pieces 1/2 cup grape tomatoes, halved
- 1/2 avocado, pitted and cubed
- 1/2 cup shredded Cheddar cheese
- 2 large flour tortillas

INSTRUCTIONS:

1. In a medium bowl, combine the lettuce, dressing, eggs, bacon, turkey, tomatoes, avocado, and cheese, and toss to combine.
2. Evenly divide the mixture onto each tortilla. Fold and roll burrito style. Slice in half and pack into lunch containers along with fruit.

HUMMUS & TURKEY WRAP

2 servings

INGREDIENTS:

- 1/4 cup hummus
- 2 large flour tortillas
- 8 slices deli turkey
- Chopped Romaine lettuce
- 1 carrot, shredded, optional
- 2 tablespoons sliced black or Kalamata olives 1/2 cup halved, grape tomatoes
- 1/2 cucumber slices
- 1 apple, sliced

INSTRUCTIONS:

1. Spread the hummus on each tortilla, top with sliced turkey, lettuce, and shredded carrots, if using, olives, and tomatoes. Fold and roll tightly before slicing in half and packing the wraps into 2 lunch containers.

APPLE & PB WRAP

2 servings

INGREDIENTS:

- 1/4 cup peanut butter or nut butter alternative
- 2 large flour tortillas
- 1/2 apple, diced
- 1/4 cup shredded carrot, optional
- 1/4 cup granola

INSTRUCTIONS:

1. Spread 2 tablespoons peanut butter over both tortillas. Top with apples, carrots, and granola. Fold and roll tightly before slicing in half and packing into lunch containers with hard-boiled eggs and fruit.

CALIFORNIA CHICKEN WRAP

2 servings

INGREDIENTS:

- 2 large flour tortillas, warmed
- 2 slices of Monterey Jack cheese
- 8-12 thin deli-style chicken slices
- A small handful of fresh spinach
- 1 small avocado, pitted and cut into slices
- 1 small Roma tomato, sliced
- 1/4 cup Ranch dressing

INSTRUCTIONS:

1. Layer the ingredients in the order given, dividing the ingredients evenly between the two tortillas.
2. Roll the tortilla up "burrito-style" around the ingredients.

To serve: Cut in half on a bias, if desired.

VEGETARIAN TACO WRAP

4 servings

INGREDIENTS:

- 4 whole grain 6-inch tortillas
- 1 cup black beans
- 1 tsp chili powder
- ½ tsp cumin
- ⅓ cup salsa
- 3 tbsp sour cream
- ½ cup grated cheddar cheese
- 4-5 romaine leaves, sliced

INSTRUCTIONS:

1. Mix black beans with chili powder and cumin.
2. To make 4 wraps, layer each wrap evenly with black beans followed by salsa and sour cream.
3. Sprinkle with grated cheese and romaine leaves.
4. Wrap tightly and slice into bite-sized pieces or leave whole.

EGG SALAD WRAP

🍴 2 servings

INGREDIENTS:
- 4 hard-boiled eggs, chopped 2 teaspoons yellow mustard 3 tablespoons mayonnaise 1/2 teaspoon salt
- 1/4 teaspoon black pepper
- 2 large flour tortillas
- 1 cup shredded Romaine lettuce or spinach

INSTRUCTIONS:
1. In a medium bowl, combine the chopped eggs, mustard, mayonnaise, salt, and pepper. Stir to combine.
2. Place the tortillas on a flat surface and top with egg salad and chopped lettuce. Fold and roll tightly before slicing in half and packing into lunch containers.

HAM & CHEESE TACOS

🍴 2 servings

INGREDIENTS:
- 8 slices deli ham
- 2 slices Cheddar cheese, halved 4 street-size flour tortillas
- Thinly slice green lettuce

INSTRUCTIONS:
1. Layer 2 slices ham and 1 slice of cheese onto each flour
2. tortillas. Top each taco with lettuce and fold.
3. Pack the tacos into lunch containers along with fruit and veggies.

ALMOND BUTTER & STRAWBERRY

2 servings

INGREDIENTS:
- 4 tablespoons almond butter or nut butter alternative
- 4 slices of sandwich bread
- 4 strawberries, thinly sliced

INSTRUCTIONS:
1. Spread the almond butter or nut-butter alternative over 2 slices of bread. Top with sliced strawberries. Assemble the sandwiches and cut each in half.
2. Pack the sandwiches into 2 lunch containers.

ENGLISH MUFFIN

2 servings

INGREDIENTS:
- 2 English muffins, halved
- 1/2 cup shredded Mozzarella cheese
- 1/2 cup halved grape tomatoes
- 4 fresh basil leaves, chopped
- Balsamic vinegar reduction

INSTRUCTIONS:
1. Preheat to 375F. Line a baking sheet with parchment paper. Place the English muffin halves on the lined baking sheet. Top with Mozzarella, tomatoes, and chopped basil. Bake for 10 minutes or until the cheese is melted and the tomatoes are slightly browned.
2. Remove from the oven and drizzle with balsamic vinegar. Divide the English muffin into 2 lunch containers and pack with fruit and veggies.

ASIAN CHICKEN WRAP

2 servings

INGREDIENTS:

Chicken Wraps:
- 2 cups cooked chicken, finely chopped
- 10-ounce can no sugar added mandarin oranges
- 2 stalks of celery, diced
- 2 cups coleslaw mix
- 2 green onions, thinly sliced
- 1/4 cup sliced almonds
- 1/2 teaspoon salt
- 1/4 teaspoon black pepper
- 2 10-inch flour tortillas
- 2 cups grapes
- 1 cup sugar snap peas

Asian Dressing:
- 1/3 cup rice vinegar
- 1/4 cup soy sauce
- 3 tablespoons sesame seeds
- 1 tablespoon brown sugar
- 2 teaspoons fresh ginger
- 1 1/2 teaspoon sesame oil
- 1 garlic clove, grated

INSTRUCTIONS:

1. In a lidded jar or medium bowl combine the dressing ingredients. Place the lid onto the jar and seal. Shake to combine. Refrigerate for up to 1 week. In a large bowl, combine the cooked chicken, mandarin oranges, celery, coleslaw mix, green onions, almonds, salt, and pepper. Add 1/2 cup of dressing and toss to combine.
2. To serve, place 1/2 cup to 3/4 cup of the chicken salad onto each tortilla. Fold in the sides and roll burrito style. Cut each wrap in half and divide between 2 lunch containers along with the fruit and veggies.

KITCHEN NOTE:
Refrigerate the remaining chicken salad in an airtight container for up to 3 days.

ITALIAN SANDWICH

2 servings

INGREDIENTS:

- 4 slices sandwich bread
- 2 tablespoons of mayonnaise 1/2 cup shredded or 2 slices of Mozzarella cheese
- 8 thin slices of salami
- Butter, for grilling

INSTRUCTIONS:

1. Place the bread onto a flat surface. Spread mayonnaise over each slice. Top 2 slices with cheese and salami. Assemble the sandwiches and butter on both sides.
2. In a large non-stick pan over medium-high heat, grill each sandwich for 3 minutes per side, or until the bread is golden brown and the cheese is melted.
3. Remove the sandwiches from heat and allow them to cool down to room temperature before cutting in half and packing them into lunch containers along with the veggies and fruit.

PESTO GRILLED CHEESE

2 servings

INGREDIENTS:

- 4 slices of sandwich bread
- 3 tablespoons pesto
- 1 grilled or cooked chicken breast, thinly sliced
- 2 slices Provolone cheese
- Butter, for grilling

INSTRUCTIONS:

1. Spread the pesto over each slice of bread and top with chicken and cheese. Close the sandwiches and butter on both sides.
2. In a large non-stick pan over medium-high heat, grill each sandwich for 3 minutes per side, or until the bread is golden brown and the cheese has melted.
3. Remove the sandwiches from heat and allow them to cool down to room temperature before cutting in half and packing them inside lunch containers along with fruit and veggies.

BREAKFAST BURRITO

4 servings

INGREDIENTS:

Breakfast Burritos:
- 6 eggs, whisked
- 4 burrito style tortillas, warmed
- 1 1/2 cups reserved Roasted Veggies
- 1/2 cup sour cream
- 1/2 cup salsa
- 1/2 cup shredded Cheddar cheese
- 2 cups strawberries, halved

Roasted Veggies:
- 1/2 pint cherry tomatoes
- 1/2 cup corn
- 1 large zucchini, diced
- 1/2 white onion sliced
- 1 red bell pepper, seeded and sliced
- 1 tablespoon olive oil
- 1/2 tablespoon taco seasoning
- 15-ounce can of black beans, drained
- Juice from half a lime

INSTRUCTIONS:

1. Preheat the oven to 400F. Line a large baking sheet with parchment paper. Add the tomatoes, corn, zucchini, onion, and bell pepper to the baking sheet. Drizzle with olive oil and season with taco seasoning. Toss to coat the veggies.
2. Bake for 15 minutes, stir and add the black beans, and a few squeezes of lime juice. Bake for another 5 to 10 minutes, until all the veggies are soft.
3. Meanwhile, in a large non-stick skillet scramble the eggs. Once the eggs are cooked through remove them from the heat.
4. Warm the tortillas in the microwave. Add the eggs, followed by the veggies, sour cream, salsa, and cheese onto the center of each tortilla. Fold and roll burrito style. Slice each wrap in half and divide into 4 lunch containers.

FALAFEL WRAP

2 servings

INGREDIENTS:

Falafels:
- 2 cups canned chickpeas, drained and rinsed
- 1 tablespoon ground cumin
- 1 teaspoon coriander, optional
- 3 garlic cloves, minced
- 1/2 cup diced white onion
- 3 tablespoons freshly squeezed lemon juice
- 1/3 cup breadcrumbs
- 3 tablespoons olive oil, to pan-fry

For Serving:
- 4 pita rounds
- 1/2 cup hummus
- Chopped Romaine lettuce
  Sliced tomato
- Feta cheese crumbles

INSTRUCTIONS:

1. In a food processor or blender, combine the chickpeas with the seasonings, garlic, onions, lemon juice, and breadcrumbs. Process until it becomes a smooth thick paste.
2. With wet hands, form dough into small balls, the size of a large walnut. Press down to form 1 1/2-inch patty. If the mixture is too sticky, add a little bit more breadcrumbs. If it's too dry, add a tablespoon or 2 of water.
3. In a large skillet, heat the oil over medium-high heat. Pan-fry the falafels for 3-4 minutes on each side, or until sides are golden brown. Remove falafel onto a paper towel-lined plate and blot excess oil with additional paper towels.
4. Spread the hummus into each pita pocket. Fill each pocket with 4 falafels, lettuce, tomatoes, and feta cheese. Pack into lunch containers.

KITCHEN NOTE:
If short on time, use store-bought frozen falafels. If none are available at your local grocery, swap the falafels for 4 ounces deli meat or 2 cups shredded chicken. Use flour tortillas wraps instead of pitas or serve the falafels over a bed of lettuce, chopped tomatoes, and cucumber.

HUMMUS MELT

2 servings

INGREDIENTS:
- 1/4 cup hummus
- 4 slices of sandwich bread
- 1 grilled or cooked chicken breast, thinly sliced
- 2 slices Provolone or Cheddar cheese
- Butter, for grilling

INSTRUCTIONS:

1. Spread the hummus over each slice of bread. Top 2 slices with chicken and cheese. Assemble the sandwiches and butter on both sides.
2. In a medium non-stick pan over medium-high heat, grill each sandwich for 2 to 3 minutes. Flip and continue to grill until the cheese is melted.
3. Remove from heat and allow the sandwiches to cool down to room temperature before slicing in half and packing into lunch containers.

APPLE & PB CRUNCH

2 servings

INGREDIENTS:
- 4 tablespoons peanut butter or nut butter alternative
- 4 slices sandwich bread
- 1 Honey Crisp or Granny Smith apple, thinly sliced
- 1 tablespoon honey

INSTRUCTIONS:
1. Spread the peanut butter over 2 slices of bread, top with the apples and a drizzle of honey. Assemble the sandwiches before slicing them in half and packing them into lunch containers.

APPLE GRILLED CHEESE

2 servings

INGREDIENTS:
- 4 slices of sandwich bread
- 2 slices of Cheddar cheese
- 1 Granny Smith apple, cored and thinly sliced
- Butter, for grilling

INSTRUCTIONS:
1. Top 2 slices of bread with cheese and apple slices. Assemble the sandwiches and butter on both sides.
2. In a large non-stick pan over medium-high heat, grill each sandwich for 3 minutes per side or until the bread is golden brown and the cheese has melted.
3. Remove the sandwiches from heat and allow them to cool down to room temperature before cutting them in half and packing them into 2 lunch containers.

EGG SALAD SANDWICH

2 servings

INGREDIENTS:
- 4 hard-boiled eggs, chopped
  2 teaspoons yellow mustard 3 tablespoons mayonnaise 1/2 teaspoon salt
- 1/4 teaspoon black pepper
- 4 slices of sandwich bread
- 1 cup chopped lettuce
- 2 cups strawberries

INSTRUCTIONS:
1. In a medium bowl, combine the chopped eggs, mustard, mayonnaise, salt, and pepper. Stir to combine. Top 2 slices of bread with the egg salad and chopped lettuce. Slice each sandwich in half and pack it into 2 lunch containers.

TOASTED HAM SANDWICH

2 servings

INGREDIENTS:
- 4 slices of sandwich bread
- 2 tablespoons mayonnaise
- 1 tablespoon Dijon mustard
- 4 slices of deli ham
- 2 slices of Cheddar cheese
- Shredded lettuce, optional

INSTRUCTIONS:
1. Lightly toast the sandwich bread. Spread a thin layer of mayonnaise and mustard onto each slice. Top with ham, cheese, and lettuce. Assemble the sandwiches.
2. Slice the sandwiches in half and pack them into 2 lunch containers.

CHICKPEA SANDWICH

2 servings

INGREDIENTS:

- 15-ounce can of chickpeas, rinsed and drained
- 2 tablespoons fresh lemon juice
- 1 tablespoon olive oil
- 1/2 cup diced red bell pepper 2 ribs celery, diced
- 1/2 teaspoon salt
- 1/2 teaspoon black pepper
- 4 slices of sandwich bread
- Shredded lettuce, for serving

INSTRUCTIONS:

1. In a medium bowl, using a fork, mash half the chickpeas. Add the remaining chickpeas, lemon juice, olive oil, bell pepper, celery, salt, and black pepper, and stir to combine.
2. If desired, toast the bread in a toaster.
3. Spread the chickpea salad mixture over 2 slices of bread, and top with lettuce, if using. Assemble the sandwiches and cut them in half.
4. Divide the sandwiches into 2 lunch containers.

VEGETABLE CLUB

2 servings

INGREDIENTS:
- 1/4 cup hummus
- 4 slices sandwich bread
- 1 tablespoon basil pesto
- 1 medium tomato, sliced thin
  1/2 cucumber, sliced
- 1/2 avocado, thinly sliced
- 2 slices Cheddar or Provolone cheese

INSTRUCTIONS:
1. Spread the hummus over 2 slices of bread and the pesto over the remaining 2 slices. Top the hummus with tomato, cucumbers, avocado, and cheese. Assemble the sandwiches and slice them in half before packing them into 2 lunch containers.

AVOCADO EGG SALAD

2 servings

INGREDIENTS:
- 1/2 avocado, peeled and pitted
- 1 tablespoon mayonnaise or Greek yogurt 1/2 tablespoon lemon juice, optional
- 1/2 teaspoon yellow mustard
- 1/4 teaspoon salt, plus more to taste
- 3 hard-boiled eggs, chopped
- 4 slices sandwich bread

INSTRUCTIONS:
1. In a medium bowl, mash the avocado until completely smooth. Add the mayonnaise or yogurt, lemon juice, mustard, and salt. Add the eggs and stir until ingredients are thoroughly mixed.
2. Add a scoop of egg salad to 2 slices of bread and assemble the sandwiches. Slice in half and pack into lunch containers.

HOMEMADE UNCRUSTABLE

2 servings

INGREDIENTS:

- 1/4 cup peanut butter or nut butter alternative
- 4 slices of sandwich bread
- 2 tablespoons
- 1/4 cup jelly, your choice 2 sliced apples
- 1 cup baby carrots

INSTRUCTIONS:

1. Spread the peanut butter onto 2 slices of bread, keeping the peanut butter in the center. Spread the jelly in the center of the remaining 2 slices and assemble the sandwiches.
2. Using a sandwich crimper or wide rimmed glass, press it into the center of the sandwich and remove the outer crust. Repeat with the remaining sandwich.
3. Pack the uncrustables into lunch containers.

KITCHEN NOTE:
Make these in batches, freezing the extra. To make it fun, use a cookie cutter.

WAFFLE SANDWICH

2 servings

INGREDIENTS:

- 4 whole-wheat waffles (or waffles of choice)
- 4 tablespoons almond or peanut butter
- 6 strawberries, sliced

INSTRUCTIONS:

1. Lightly toast the waffles in a toaster or toaster oven. Spread 1 tablespoon of almond or peanut butter over each waffle.
2. Top 2 waffles with sliced strawberries and assemble the sandwiches. Slice each waffle sandwich in half and divide it into 2 lunch containers.

HAWAIIAN SLIDERS

2 servings

INGREDIENTS:
- 4 Hawaiian rolls
- 2 teaspoons yellow mustard
- 2 tablespoons mayonnaise
- 4 slices deli ham
- 2 slices Swiss cheese, halved 2 fresh pineapple rings, halved 1 cup strawberries
- 1 cup baby carrots

INSTRUCTIONS:
1. Halve the Hawaiian rolls and place onto a flat surface. Spread the mustard over 2 halves and the mayonnaise over the remaining halves. Top 4 halves with ham, cheese, and pineapple slices. Assemble the sliders and pack into lunch containers with fruit and veggies.

KITCHEN NOTE:
We recommend using fresh pineapple, instead of canned. If using canned, pat dry with a paper towel to avoid excess moisture. Use any leftover pineapple to serve with another lunch later in the week.

CAPRESE SLIDERS

2 servings

INGREDIENTS:
- 2 tablespoons pesto
- 4 whole wheat rolls or Hawaiian rolls
- 4 Roma tomato slices
- 1/3 cup shredded Mozzarella cheese

INSTRUCTIONS:
1. Halve each roll and spread the pesto over each half. Top 4 halves with the tomato and cheese. Assemble the sliders and pack into lunch containers.

PITA PIZZA

2 servings

INGREDIENTS:

- 2 pita rounds
- 1/2 cup pizza sauce
- 1/4 cup feta cheese
- 1 bell pepper, sliced
- 2 tablespoons sliced black olives

INSTRUCTIONS:

1. Position the oven rack in the middle of the oven. Preheat the oven to 400F.
2. Place the pitas onto the baking sheet, spread the pizza sauce over each pita, and top with feta cheese, bell pepper, and olives.
3. Bake for 7 minutes, until cheese, is bubbly and melted. Remove from oven and allow to cool down to room temperature before packing the pizzas into lunch containers.

KITCHEN NOTE:
Turn this pita pizza into a pizza wrap or quesadilla. Spread the marinara sauce over 2 tortillas, top with cheese, and pepperoni slices. Fold and roll burrito-style.

HUMMUS & TURKEY

2 servings

INGREDIENTS:
- 1/4 cup hummus
- 2 pita rounds, halved
- 6 slices of deli turkey
- 2 slices Provolone cheese, halved 1/4-pint grape tomatoes, halved Chopped Romaine lettuce
- 2 apples, sliced

INSTRUCTIONS:
1. Spread the hummus inside each pita pocket. Fill each half with turkey, cheese, tomatoes, and lettuce. Pack the pitas into lunch containers along with fruit.

CHICKEN PITA

2 servings

INGREDIENTS:
- 2 pita rounds, halved
- 1/4 cup hummus
- 8-ounce grilled chicken breast, sliced 1/2 cup halved grape tomatoes
- 1/4 cup sliced black olives
- Shredded lettuce, optional

INSTRUCTIONS:
1. Open each pita pocket and spread with hummus. Fill each pocket with the cooked chicken, tomatoes, olives, and lettuce.

BLT LETTUCE WRAP

2 servings

INGREDIENTS:
- 1/4 cup ranch dressing
- 4 whole Iceberg lettuce leaves
- 4 slices of cooked bacon, chopped
- 1/2 cup halved cherry tomatoes

INSTRUCTIONS:
1. Drizzle 1 tablespoon of ranch dressing over each lettuce leaf. Divide chopped bacon and grape tomatoes among the lettuce leaves. Fold into a closed "cup" and insert 2 per lunch container.

TURKEY & CHEESE LETTUCE WRAP

2 servings

INGREDIENTS:

- 4 large Boston Bibb lettuce leaves 1 tomato, sliced
- 4 slices of deli turkey
- 2 slices Provolone cheese, halved Pickles
- 1 tablespoon mustard

INSTRUCTIONS:

1. Layer one lettuce leaf on top of the other to create 2 "cups".
2. Layer the tomatoes, turkey, cheese, and pickles onto each lettuce cup. Drizzle with mustard.
3. Roll the lettuce wrap tightly and slice in half before packing it into a glass lunch container.

ASIAN CHICKEN LETTUCE WRAP

2 servings

INGREDIENTS:

Chicken Wraps
- 2 cups cooked chicken, finely chopped
- 10-ounce can no sugar added mandarin oranges
- 2 stalks celery, diced
- 2 cups coleslaw mix
- 2 green onions, thinly sliced
- 1/4 cup sliced almonds
- 1/2 teaspoon salt
- 1/4 teaspoon black pepper
- 1 head Iceberg lettuce, outer leaves removed

Asian Dressing:
- 1/3 cup rice vinegar
- 1/4 cup soy sauce
- 3 tablespoons sesame seeds
- 1 tablespoon brown sugar
- 2 teaspoons fresh ginger
- 1 1/2 teaspoon sesame oil
- 1 garlic clove, grated

INSTRUCTIONS:

1. In a lidded jar or medium bowl combine the dressing ingredients. Place the lid onto the jar and seal. Shake to combine. Refrigerate for up to 1 week.
2. In a large bowl, combine the cooked chicken, mandarin oranges, celery, coleslaw mix, green onions, almonds, salt, and pepper. Add 1/2 cup of dressing and toss to combine.
3. To serve, layer 1 lettuce leaf on top another to create a sturdy base. Repeat with remaining lettuce until you have 4 lettuce cups. Fill each cup with chicken salad and pack into lunch containers.

KITCHEN NOTE:
Refrigerate the remaining chicken salad in an airtight container for up to 3 days

BLACK BEAN QUESADILLA

2 servings

INGREDIENTS:
- 1/2 cup canned black beans
- 1/4 cup frozen corn, thawed
- 1 tablespoon chopped cilantro
- 1 teaspoon taco seasoning
- 2 large flour tortillas
- 1/2 cup shredded Cheddar cheese
- Butter, for grilling

INSTRUCTIONS:
1. In a medium bowl, combine the black beans, corn, cilantro, and taco seasoning. Top 1 tortilla with the black bean and corn mixture, cheese, and remaining tortilla.
2. In a large skillet, melt butter over medium-high heat. Place the quesadillas in the skillet and cook until the cheese begins to melt, about 2 minutes. Flip and grill for another 2 minutes or until the cheese is completely melted.
3. Remove from the skillet and allow to cool to room temperature before slicing and dividing into 2 lunch containers.

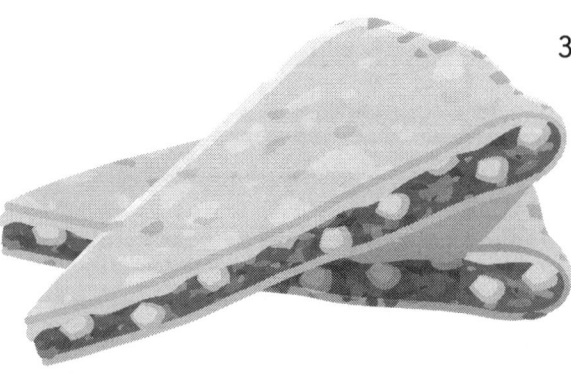

FRUIT & CHEDDAR QUESADILLA

2 servings

INGREDIENTS:

- 2 large flour tortillas
- 1 small pear, sliced thin
- 1/2 cup shredded Cheddar cheese
- Butter, for grilling

INSTRUCTIONS:

1. In a medium bowl, combine the black beans, corn, cilantro, and taco seasoning. Top 1 tortilla with the black bean and corn mixture, cheese, and remaining tortilla.
2. In a large skillet, melt butter over medium-high heat. Place the quesadillas in the skillet and cook until the cheese begins to melt, about 2 minutes. Flip and grill for another 2 minutes or until the cheese is completely melted.
3. Remove from the skillet and allow to cool to room temperature before slicing and dividing into 2 lunch containers.

BUFFALO SLIDERS

4 servings

INGREDIENTS:

- 1-pound boneless, skinless chicken breasts
- 1 cup Buffalo sauce
- 8 pretzel rolls, halved
- 1/2 cup blue cheese crumbles
- 4 slices Provolone cheese, halved Shredded lettuce

INSTRUCTIONS:

1. Place the chicken breasts into the dish of a slow cooker. Pour the buffalo sauce over the chicken and stir to combine. Cover and cook on low for 7 to 8 hours or high for 4 to 5 hours.
2. Once the chicken is cooked through, shred the meat with 2 forks and toss to coat with the sauce.
3. Place the rolls, open-face on a flat surface. Top 8 halves with Buffalo chicken, Blue cheese crumbles, Provolone cheese, and lettuce, and assemble the sliders.
4. Pack the sliders into lunch containers.

SALMON SALAD PITA

🍴 4 servings

INGREDIENTS:

- 2 5-ounce cans salmon, drained 2 tablespoons mayonnaise
- 1/2 cup diced celery
- 1 teaspoon lemon juice
- 1/2 teaspoon cumin
- 1/2 teaspoon salt
- 1/2 teaspoon black pepper
- 4 pita rounds, halved
- Chopped Romaine lettuce

INSTRUCTIONS:

1. In a large bowl, add the salmon meat and use a fork to break up larger pieces into smaller flake-like pieces. Add the mayonnaise, diced celery, lemon juice, cumin, salt, and pepper to the bowl and stir to combine.
2. Open each pita half and fill with a layer of lettuce. Divide the salmon salad into the pita pockets and pack it into lunch containers.

CHEESE & APPLE QUESADILLA

4 servings

INGREDIENTS:

- 2 large flour tortillas
- 1 small apple, sliced thin
- 1/2 cup shredded Cheddar cheese
- Butter, for grilling

INSTRUCTIONS:

1. Place the tortillas onto a flat surface. Top one tortilla with the apple slices and Cheddar cheese. Assemble the quesadilla.
2. In a large skillet, melt the butter over medium-high heat. Place the quesadillas in the skillet and cook until the cheese begins to melt about 2 minutes. Flip and grill for another 2 minutes or until the cheese is completely melted.
3. Remove from the skillet and allow the quesadillas to cool down to room temperature before slicing and packing into 2 lunch containers.

BUFFALO QUESADILLA

4 servings

INGREDIENTS:
- 1 pounds boneless, skinless chicken breasts
- 1/2 cup Buffalo sauce
- 2 large flour tortillas
- 1/2 cup shredded Mozzarella cheese Butter, for grilling
- 2 cups celery sticks
- 1/4 cup ranch dressing

INSTRUCTIONS:

1. Place the chicken in the dish of a slow cooker, top with Buffalo sauce and toss to coat. Cover and set on low for 8 hours or high for 5 hours.
2. Once the chicken is cooked through and easily shreds apart between 2 forks shred the meat in the slow cooker dish and toss to coat with the sauce.
3. Top 1 tortilla with the Buffalo chicken, cheese, and remaining quesadilla.
4. In a large skillet, melt butter over medium-high heat. Place the quesadilla into the skillet and grill for 3 minutes or until the cheese begins to melt. Flip and grill for another 3 minutes or until the cheese is completely melted. Remove from the skillet and allow to cool down to room temperature before slicing into 6 triangles.
5. Divide the quesadillas between 2 lunch containers.

BITE SIZED LUNCHES

QUINOA & CHEESE

4-6 servings

INGREDIENTS:

- 1 1/2 cups cooked quinoa
- 1 cup shredded Monterrey Jack or Mozzarella Cheese
- 1/4 cup grated Parmesan cheese 1 teaspoon Italian seasoning
- 1/2 teaspoon garlic powder
- 1/4 teaspoon salt
- 1 large egg, whisked
- 1 cup baby carrots
- Marinara sauce, for dipping

INSTRUCTIONS:

1. Preheat the oven to 400F and grease or spray a mini muffin pan.
2. In a large bowl, combine quinoa, grated cheese, grated Parmesan cheese, Italian seasonings, garlic powder, salt and stir to combine. Add the whisked egg and mix until all ingredients are incorporated.
3. Spoon the quinoa mixture into the mini muffin pan.
4. Bake for 15-18 minutes until the tops are golden brown. Remove from oven and allow bites to cool down to room temperature before packing 6 bites into each lunch container.
5. Fill the small lidded sauce containers with marinara sauce and pack along with the mini quiches.

MINI PIZZA

2 servings

INGREDIENTS:

- 6 eggs
- 3 tablespoons milk
- 1/4 cup pepperoni slices, chopped
- 1 cup shredded Mozzarella cheese

INSTRUCTIONS:

1. Preheat the oven to 350F and grease a 24-count mini muffin pan.
2.
3. In a large bowl, whisk the eggs and milk. Add the pepperoni and shredded cheese. Mix to combine all the ingredients.
4. Distribute the egg mixture evenly into the muffin pan cups. Bake in the preheated oven 15 to 18 minutes, until the tops are puffy and the egg mixture has cooked through. Remove from the oven and allow the quiches to cool in the pan before removing them with a small knife or spatula.
5. Place 4 to 6 mini quiches into each lunch container.

HAM & CHEESE QUICHES

4 servings

INGREDIENTS:

- 6 eggs
- 3 tablespoons of milk
- 4 slices deli ham, chopped
- 1 cup shredded Mozzarella cheese

KITCHEN NOTE:
This recipe yields 24 mini quiches. Leftovers will keep up to 4 days, refrigerated in an airtight container.

INSTRUCTIONS:

1. Preheat the oven to 350F. Grease a 24-cup mini muffin pan.
2. In a medium bowl, whisk the eggs with the milk. Add the ham and cheese, and whisk to combine.
3. Using a large spoon or measuring cup, ladle the egg mixture into the mini muffin cups.
4. Place in the preheated oven and bake for 10 to
5. 12 minutes or until the tops are lightly browned.
6. Remove from the oven and allow to cool before
7. Remove the mini quiches with a knife or spatula. Allow to cool down to room temperature
8. before packing 4 to 5 mini quiches into lunch containers.

SPINACH & BACON QUICHES

🍴 4-6 servings

INGREDIENTS:

- 6 eggs
- 3 tablespoons milk
- 3/4 cup spinach, finely chopped
- 1 cup shredded Cheddar cheese
- 4 strips bacon, cooked and chopped
- 1/2 teaspoon black pepper

KITCHEN NOTE:
This recipe yields 24 mini quiches. Leftovers make an awesome breakfast or quick snack! Keep refrigerated and enjoy for up to 4 days.

INSTRUCTIONS:

1. Preheat the oven to 350F and grease a 24-count mini muffin pan.
2. In a large bowl, whisk together the eggs and milk. Add in the spinach, cheese, bacon, and black pepper, and stir to combine.
3. Distribute egg mixture evenly into muffin cups. Bake for 15 to 18 minutes.
4. Once cooked, allow the mini quiches to cool in the pan before carefully removing them with a small knife or spatula. Pack 4 to 6 mini quiches in a lunch container along with your choice of fruit and veggies.

SUSHI FRIED RICE BALLS

4 servings

INGREDIENTS:

- 1 cup sushi rice, rinsed, drained
- 1/2 cup frozen peas and corn
- 60g sliced ham, finely chopped
- 2 green onions, thinly sliced
- 1/4 cup sushi seasoning
- Salt-reduced soy sauce, to serve

INSTRUCTIONS:

1. Cook rice following packet directions. Transfer to a large bowl.
2. Meanwhile, place frozen vegetables in a heatproof bowl. Cover with boiling water. Stand for 2 minutes. Drain. Refresh under cold water.
3. Add vegetables, ham, onion, and seasoning to rice. Stir until well combined. Spread over a large tray lined with baking paper. Set aside to cool.
4. Using damp hands, roll level tablespoons of rice mixture into balls. Place on a tray lined with baking paper. Serve with soy sauce or freeze until required (see notes).

KITCHEN NOTE:
Make ahead: Balls can be frozen for up to 1 month. Place cooked balls in 1 layer on a tray. Freeze for 4 hours or until firm. Transfer to a snap-lock bag and return to the freezer. Thaw balls in the fridge overnight. Serve reheated in the microwave or at room temperature.

TURKEY PINWHEEL

🍴 2 servings

INGREDIENTS:

- 3 tablespoons pesto
- 2 large flour tortillas
- 6 slices of deli turkey
- 1 small tomato, sliced
- 2 slices provolone cheese

INSTRUCTIONS:

1. Spread the pesto over each tortilla. Top with turkey, tomatoes, and provolone. Roll up the tortilla tightly.
2. Slice each roll into 1-inch wheels, about 8 per roll.
3. Divide the pinwheels between 2 lunch containers.

KITCHEN NOTE:
Freeze leftover pesto in a zip bag for future use.

MINI TACO HAND PIES

6-8 servings

INGREDIENTS:

- 1 box refrigerated pie dough (14.1 oz)
- 3/4 lb ground beef
- 1 teaspoon olive oil
- 1/2 teaspoon salt
- 3/4 teaspoon chili powder
- 3/4 teaspoon paprika
- 3/4 teaspoon onion powder
- 3/4 teaspoon garlic powder
- 3/4 teaspoon cumin
- 1/2 cup black beans
- 1/4 cup shredded cheddar cheese
- 1 egg, lightly beaten
- 1/2 teaspoon water

INSTRUCTIONS:

1. Heat olive oil in a large skillet over medium heat. Add ground beef, stir to crumble. Add salt, chili powder, paprika, onion powder, garlic powder, and cumin; stir. Continue to cook until beef is no longer pink and seasoning has been incorporated. This should take 8-10 minutes. The beef mixture should thicken as it cooks. Stir in black beans, remove from heat and set aside to cool.
2. Preheat oven to 425. Sprinkle flour over a work surface. Roll out one sheet of dough. Cut dough into circles using a 3-inch biscuit cutter, rerolling scraps as necessary. Repeat with remaining sheet of dough.
3. Arrange half of the circles on a baking sheet that has been sprayed with cooking spray. Place a tablespoon of meat mixture on the dough circles, top with roughly a half teaspoon of cheese. Place the other circle halves over the meat and cheese mixture.
4. Pinch edges together with the tines of a fork.
5. Combine egg and water in a bowl. Brush egg wash over the top of each hand pie.
6. Bake in the oven for 13-15 minutes or just until golden. Remove from oven and let hand pies cool slightly before serving. Serve with your favorite taco fixings on the side.
7. Store hand pies in the refrigerator in an air-tight container or a zip-top bag.

BACON & AVOCADO PINWHEEL

🍴 2 servings

INGREDIENTS:

- 1/2 avocado, mashed
- 2 large flour tortillas or wraps
- 4 slices bacon, cooked and crumbled
- 1/4 cup shredded Mozzarella cheese

INSTRUCTIONS:

1. Spread the mashed avocado onto both tortillas. Top with bacon and shredded cheese. Roll tightly and slice into 1-inch rounds.
2. Divide and pack the pinwheels into 2 lunch containers.

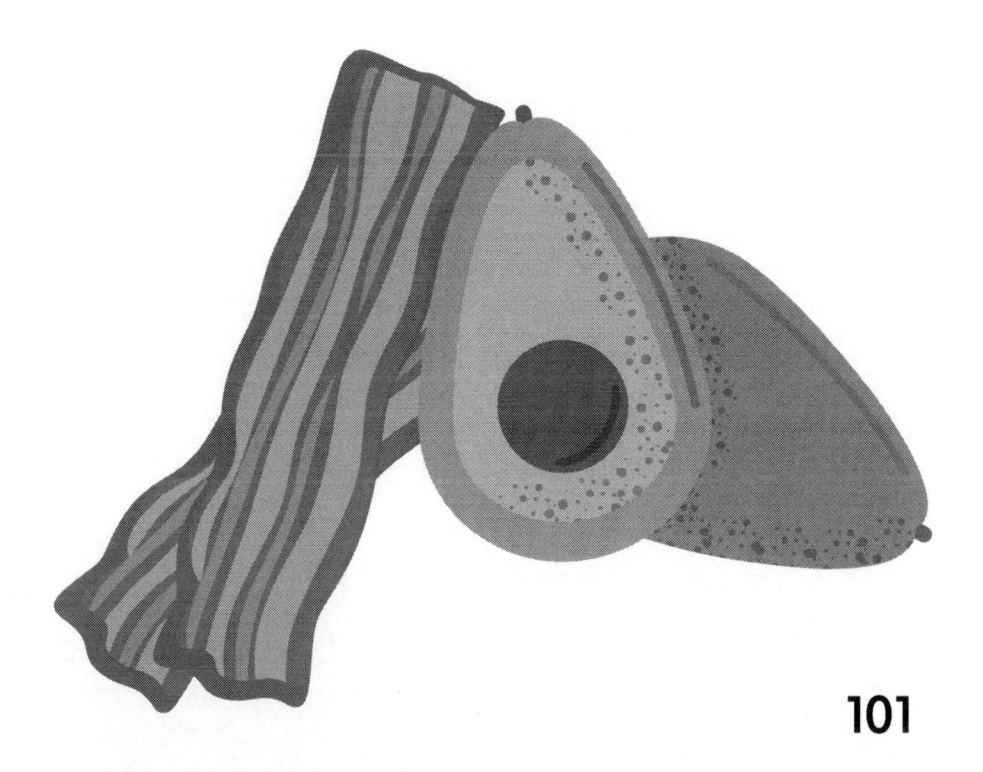

GUAC DEVILLED EGGS

🍴 2 servings

INGREDIENTS:

- 4 hard-boiled eggs
- 1/4 cup guacamole
- 1 tablespoon shredded Cheddar cheese

INSTRUCTIONS:

1. Halve the eggs lengthwise, carefully remove the yolks, and place them into a small bowl. Mash the egg yolks with a fork and add the guacamole and cheese. Stir to combine until smooth.
2. With a spoon, scoop the egg mixture inside each egg white. Divide the deviled eggs between 2 lunch containers.

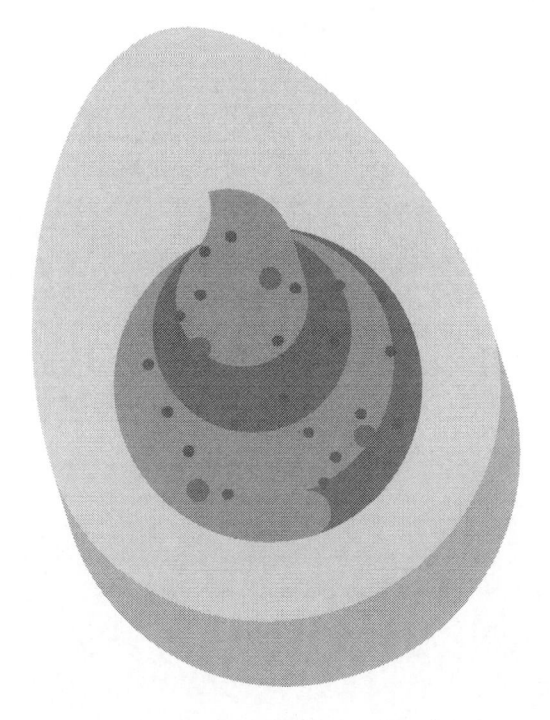

MUFFIN-PAN FRIED RICE CUPS

🍴 4-6 servings

INGREDIENTS:

- 1 cup brown rice
- 2 tsp extra virgin olive oil
- 1 small brown onion, finely chopped
- 2 shortcut bacon rashers, trimmed, finely chopped
- 12 square wonton wrappers
- 1/2 cup frozen peas
- 300g can corn kernels, drained
- 2 tbsp hoisin sauce
- 3 eggs, lightly beaten

INSTRUCTIONS:

1. Cook rice following the absorption method on the packet. Transfer to a heatproof bowl.
2. Meanwhile, heat oil in a frying pan over medium-high heat. Add onion. Cook for 5 minutes or until softened. Add bacon. Cook for 5 minutes or until golden. Add to rice. Set aside for 10 minutes to cool.
3. Preheat oven to 425 F. Grease a 12-hole (1/3-cup-capacity) muffin pan. Line holes with wonton wrappers.
4. Add peas, corn, hoisin sauce, and egg to the rice mixture. Season with pepper. Stir to combine. Spoon mixture into prepared pan holes, pressing to compact. Bake for 20 to 22 minutes or until golden and just firm to touch.
5. Stand in pan for 10 minutes. Using a butter knife, carefully lift cups from the pan and transfer them to a wire rack to cool completely. Once cold, wrap individually in plastic wrap, then foil. Freeze for up to 2 months. Remove foil and place it in a lunchbox.

SIDES & SNACKS

WHOLE FOOD SIDES

- Carrots
- Bell peppers, sliced
- Cucumbers, sliced
- Cherry/grape tomatoes
- Snap peas
- Celery
- Edamame
- Apples
- Grapes
- Berries
- Peaches
- Mango
- Oranges
- Pineapple
- Melon
- Banana
- Hard-boiled eggs
- Greek/plain yogurt
- Deli meat

PANTRY SIDES

- Nuts and seeds
- Nut butter and nut-free alternative
- Dried fruit, in moderation
- Jerky, minimally processed
- Olives
- Pickles

HOMEMADE SIDES

- Hummus
- Pantry Granola
- Easy Guacamole
- Homemade Salsa
- Energy Bites
- Smoothies
- Homemade Fruit Leather
- Healthy Breakfast Cookies
- Hummus Stuffed Celery

STORE-BOUGHT

- RX Bar
- That's It Real Fruit Bar
- Blue Diamond Almonds
- Moon Cheese Snacks
- StarKist Tuna Packs
- Beef Jerky
- Justin's Classic Almond Butter
- Seaweed Snacks
- Bare Baked Snacks

Printed in Great Britain
by Amazon